# HOW WASHINGTON WORKS

# HOW WASHINGTON WORKS
## The Executive's Guide to Government

A. LEE FRITSCHLER
BERNARD H. ROSS

*1817*

## HARPER BUSINESS
A Division of Harper & Row Publishers, New York

*Grand Rapids, Philadelphia, St. Louis, San Francisco*
*London, Singapore, Sydney, Tokyo, Toronto*

International Standard Book Number: 0–88730–079–0 (cloth)
0–88730–454–0 (paper)

Library of Congress Catalog Card Number: 86–32265

Printed in the United States of America

**Library of Congress Cataloging-in-Publication Data**

Fritschler, A. Lee, 1937-
How Washington works.

(Ballinger series in business and public policy)
Includes index.
1. Business and politics — United States.
2. United States — Politics and government.
I. Ross, Bernard H., 1934-      II. Title.
III. Series.
JK 467.F745   1987      322'.3'0973      86–32265
ISBN 0–88730–079–0 (cloth)
ISBN 0–88730–454–0 (paper)
90 91 92 93 HC 10 9 8 7 6 5 4 3 2 1

For

*Susan*
*Craig, Katherine, and Eric*

and

*Marlene*
*Jeffrey, Joanne, and Carolyn*

# CONTENTS

List of Figures and Tables                                      xi

Preface                                                        xiii


Chapter 1
Business-Government Relations
In the United States                                             1

Sources of Antagonism                                           1
A Paradoxical Relationship                                      2
New Corporate Functions                                        3
A Changing Corporate Environment                               4
Constitutional Restraints on Government Management             5
Improving the Executive's Understanding of Government          7


Chapter 2
Public and Private Sectors:
Differences and Similarities                                    9

The Underlying Differences                                      10
Difficulties of Public Management                               16
Defining Objectives                                             19

## Chapter 3
## Regulations and Responses                                    23

Two Classes of Government Regulation                            24
Business Support for Regulation I                               36
Business Problems with Regulation II                           38
The Complicated Politics of Deregulation                       39


## Chapter 4
## The Other Side of the Coin:
## Business-Government Cooperation                               43

The Roots of Government Support                                 44
Government Activity on Behalf of Business                       46
Industrial Policy: Pros and Cons                               50
Existing and Proposed Industrial Policies                       52


## Chapter 5
## The Management and Managers
## of Government                                                 57

How Many and Where?                                            57
Civil Service Reforms                                          61
Comparing Benefits                                             63
Bureaucracy under Attack                                       65


## Chapter 6
## Decisionmaking Systems and
## the Corporate Lobbyist                                        69

Defining Program Interests                                      70
Components of Decisionmaking Systems                           71
Important Characteristics of Decisionmaking Systems            73
The Role of Congress in Decisionmaking                         76
Washington Lobbyists                                           81
Business Political Action Committees                            87

Chapter 7
**Managing the Decisionmaking Systems:
Administrative Agencies and the Executive
Office of the President**                                    93

Rulemaking in Administrative Agencies              94
Hearings in the Agencies                           97
The Executive Office of the President             100
The Office of Management and Budget               104


Chapter 8
**The Decisionmaking Systems
in Operation**                                    107

How to Locate Decisionmaking Systems              107
Tracking Decisionmaking Systems                   110
Decisionmaking Systems in Action                  112
Initiating Change in the Decisionmaking Systems   115


Chapter 9
**Strengths and Weaknesses: A Critique of
Government Decisionmaking Systems**               123

Pluralism, Bargaining, and Incrementalism         124
Government's Response to Big Issues                127
Improving Government Decisionmaking               134
Congress and the Budget                           136


Chapter 10
**Business and Government
in the Future**                                   141

An Expanding Federal Role in the Economy          142
Fifteen Years of Deregulation                     143
Protectionism and Industrial Policy               145

## Appendixes

A — How a Bill Becomes Law    153
B — How to Use the *Federal Register*    165
C — How to Use the *Code of Federal Regulations*    169
D — Rules and Regulations for Registering as a Lobbyist    173
E — Rules and Regulations Governing the Creation of
    Political Action Committees    177

Suggestions for Further Reading    181

Index    189

About the Authors    197

# LIST OF FIGURES AND TABLES

**Figures**

| | | |
|---|---|---|
| 6-1 | A Government Decisionmaking System | 71 |
| 7-1 | Know Your Federal Regulations | 96 |
| 8-1 | A Government Decisionmaking System | 111 |
| 9-1 | U.S. Foreign Trade Decisionmaking | 132 |
| A-1 | How a Bill Becomes Law | 160 |

**Tables**

| | | |
|---|---|---|
| 3-1 | Economic and Social Regulation: Major Regulatory Programs by Year of Birth, 1863 to Date | 27 |
| 3-2 | Selected Major Deregulatory Actions, 1970–85 | 34 |
| 5-1 | Government Employment and Population, 1955–85 | 59 |
| 5-2 | Public Sector Employment as of October 1984 | 60 |
| 6-1 | Largest PAC Contributors, 1983–84 Elections | 88 |
| 10-1 | Levels of Corporate Involvement in Public Policy Issues | 148 |

# PREFACE

Government has become a major element of the environment in which America's business executives operate. Government spending decisions and regulations shape and even change executives' decisions on what is produced, who produces it, and how it is produced and distributed. Thus, executives stand to gain much in learning how government makes decisions on spending—both increases and cutbacks—and how it decides which policies—public or private—are to be altered and which are not.

In contemporary government-business relations these facts are clear:

- Government decisions affect many management decisions made by corporate executives.

- Business executives spend more time on government matters each year.

- Government not only regulates business but supports it in a variety of ways and has become its single biggest customer.

Through issuing numerous rewards and penalties, government can manipulate the environment in which business operates. Government spending for research, development, and contracting amounts to tens of billions of dollars annually. Most major industries operating today were started as a result of some important government decisions. Aircraft manufacturing, airlines, computers, road and rail transportation, and a wide variety of space-age industries were launched direct-ly or stimulated by government actions.

This book provides business executives and students of business with the knowledge and understanding they need to operate in a complex and changing government environment. Business executives will be able to identify those decisionmaking systems that affect their corporate or industry interests. Using this information, they can make sound judgments and take the necessary steps to ensure that their corporations' interests are fully and fairly represented in the decisionmaking process. They will find out:

- How government decisions are made.

- How a business executive can navigate the system.

- What the major similarities and differences are between public- and private-sector management.

- How government regulations are developed and who develops them.

- How government supports business and what some of those programs are.

- How to identify the powerful government actors in a variety of decisions areas.

- What the prospects are for reforming government decisionmaking systems.

*How Washington Works* contains an abundance of useful information on the size and structure of the public service, the types of people who work for government and what motivates them, and various reform proposals recently implemented or under discussion. A major section describes the differences between management in government and management in business. Business-government relations in the United States have been characterized in part by a debate between business and government executives over which business management techniques should be transferred into government operations. This book evaluates the prospects for implementing more business techniques in government and analyzes those techniques already in use.

The appendices provide practical and detailed information on:

- How a bill becomes a law.

- How to use the *Federal Register* and the *Code of Federal Regulations.*

- How to register as a lobbyist.
- How to form a political action committee.

*How Washington Works* is a complete revision of our earlier book, *Executive's Guide to Government: How Washington Works*, published in 1980, as the Reagan administration was coming into office. With that administration's pledge to reduce the role of government, one might assume that the intensity of business-government relations has diminished. This has not, however, been the case.

Major issues confronting decisionmakers in Washington today were not on the public agenda in 1980. Tax reform, budget deficits, economic sanctions against South Africa, and international trade deficits have all emerged since that time. Consequently, business executives have not only continued their high level of interest in decisionmaking in government, but they have also become more involved with policymaking at the state and local levels.

It is our belief that the question of whether or not to be represented in Washington has become moot for most successful large corporations. They know that, whether they open their own Washington office or hire an organization to represent them, their corporation—all of business, for that matter—and government are inextricably linked. There is scarcely a major issue being discussed in Washington today that does not have serious implications for one or more industries.

Over the years, we have developed and administered executive training programs for both private- and public-sector officials. In these programs we have expanded our knowledge of the policymaking process and how it responds to the interests of business. We have also had the opportunity to discuss the process with thousands of corporate executives, who have increased our understanding of the business perspective on government decisionmaking. We would like to thank several people who were especially helpful in the past few years.

Stanley L. Kroder, Frank C. Parson, Jim Geoghegan, Ken Thornton, Jim O'Malley, Cary Smith, Scotty Walsh, and Jack Sprague of IBM; Bruce Kasson and Pete Dillingham of Cray Research; and John Dillon, Ed Specht, and Larry Cohen of General Electric all shed light on the special relationship between business and government. We would also like to thank George C. Lodge and J. Ronald Fox of the Harvard Business School, Andrew W. Boesel of the U.S. Office of Personnel Management, Susan J. Tolchin of George Washington University, and Charles H. Levine and Walter Oleszek of the Congressional Research Service of the U.S. Library of Congress.

Charles E. McKittrick, Jr., vice president for governmental programs of the IBM Corporation, was instrumental in the creation of the executive development program for business executives at American University. His commitment to executive development and his professional and intellectual interest in the processes of government decisionmaking were important to us as we wrote this book.

The manuscript was read by Edwin M. Epstein of the School of Business Administration, University of California, Berkeley, Barbara D. Littell and Nancy D. Davidson of the Brookings Institution, and Murray Comarow and Bernard Rosen of American University. Their comments and suggestions improved the manuscript greatly.

Other colleagues, through their writings and comments, have also assisted us to clarify our thoughts and better understand this complex system. We especially want to thank James A. Thurber, John D. Young, and Cornelius Kerwin, all on the faculty of the College of Public and International Affairs at American University.

Thanks also to James J. Murray III, who encouraged us to write the first edition of this book and who published it while he was president of Winthrop Publishers, Inc. He is now an executive with the American Council on Education.

Tricia Patterson was an extremely helpful research assistant who saved us much time and was always available to track down missing data.

The manuscript was processed by Cheryl M. Payne and Evelyn Costelloe. A special debt of gratitude is owed to Dean Dorothy B. James of the School of Government and Public Administration at American University for fostering a climate conducive to scholarly research and for finding the resources to support that commitment.

Our developmental editor, Barbara Roth of Ballinger, maintained her sense of humor throughout and never complained about deadlines, but rather encouraged us to keep writing. Our copy editor, Cynthia Reed, kept us honest.

Washington, D.C.                                    A. Lee Fritschler
Fall 1986                                          Bernard H. Ross

# HOW WASHINGTON WORKS

# 1 BUSINESS-GOVERNMENT RELATIONS IN THE UNITED STATES

Corporate executives have good reason to be concerned with government. It has become a significant force—and not always a negative one—in the business environment. Government regulations shape and alter decisions on what is produced, how and where production occurs, who is hired or fired, and how products are distributed. Not surprisingly, as government has become increasingly involved in private-sector management, distrust and antagonism between them have grown.

## SOURCES OF ANTAGONISM

The antagonism stems from specific regulations as well as general policies that seem to be antibusiness, and from the ways in which both are carried out. Government management processes can be complex, baffling, and often contradictory. Government goals are different from those of business and more loosely defined. Management that strives to achieve political and social mandates instead of production and marketing goals seems ambiguous and even pointless to business executives. These differences feed a climate of confusion and mistrust between the two sectors.

Business executives have an outlook different from their government counterparts. They respond to opportunities in markets; government, on the other hand, intervenes in markets and shapes them to fit social and political demands. Government can limit market access, dictate nonmarket safety and quality standards, and skew markets to direct resources to groups that would otherwise not receive them. In the United States market forces usually prevail over the long term. For example, regulated industries become deregulated and safety standards become a part of customer demand. Yet the confrontation between market forces and government is a continuing, difficult, and frustrating fact of life for business executives.

Business historian Alfred Chandler wrote about a U.S. businessman who summed up his own feelings about government, and probably those of his colleagues, by saying: "Why is it that I and my American colleagues are being commonly taken to court—made to stand trial—for activities for which our counterparts in Britain and other countries of Europe are knighted or given peerages or comparable honors?"[1] This statement is perhaps an exaggeration, but it underscores both the differences between the United States and other countries and the frustrations felt by executives in this country.

## A PARADOXICAL RELATIONSHIP

These frustrations are only a part of the story. The business-government relationship is further complicated by the dependency that has developed between the two adversaries. A paradox in business-government relations is that government regulates business, and reshapes markets in curious ways, yet government also subsidizes, encourages, and protects business. Regulations create a safe environment for business. For example, without patents and contracts, banking and currency regulations, or purity certification for food and drugs, some elements of business might well collapse. The government also provides technical assistance, funds, and contracts to start new companies, to protect some businesses from foreign competition, and to bail out others that are close to bankruptcy. Government encourages economic growth by adopting fiscal and monetary policies that attempt to strengthen the economy and smooth out extreme fluctuations in business cycles.

Business executives have strong reasons to be simultaneously close to yet distant from government. Government policies can dramatically affect the success or failure of business enterprises. There are many reasons for criticizing government, but government's support of business has been an important part of our system from colonial times. Our earliest businessmen were more pragmatic in their relations with government than their counterparts seem to be today:

> To these men the new phrase "laissez-faire" probably represented a meaningless doctrine. Rather, they stood for dispersed private activity when the capital required was within the grasp of the individual, state initiative when the capital required was too great for a small group of individuals, and at all times, public policy favorable to maximum exploitation of economic opportunities with minimum capital expenditure.[2]

These early capitalists set a pattern that has persisted for 200 years. What has changed in the last five decades is the intensity of government involvement in the economy, with social and political goals having become a required component of corporate decisionmaking.

Further complicating corporate decisionmaking today is the fact that governments—national, state, and local—spend over one-third of the gross national product each year. These expenditures shape the general economic climate and specific markets for some industries. The federal government alone spends about $200 billion a year in purchases from U.S. companies. The addition of state and local government purchases substantially increases that amount. For several corporations government has become a major customer; for some it is the largest customer.


## NEW CORPORATE FUNCTIONS

The increased role of government in corporate life over the last several years has caused corporations to add new functions to executive management and in some cases to reorganize management structures altogether. Many have elevated their government relations functions to the corporate management level.

George Steiner found that CEOs spend from 25 to 50 percent of their time on external matters, including government relations. These figures are a substantial change from the late 1960s, when CEOs spent little time on external affairs. Reginald Jones, the CEO of

General Electric from 1972 to 1980, has made this plea to his fellow executives:

> Business executives must participate personally in the formation of public policy. This is not something we can delegate to our trade associations. We must study the issues, develop constructive positions, and then speak out—in public forums, in Congressional testimony, in personal contacts with our representatives in government. This is an unavoidable responsibility of business leadership today, for companies large and small.[3]

In the past business often handled government relations in a chaotic, unplanned, and reactive manner uncharacteristic of good systematic corporate management. Not so today—"issues management" is finding its way into corporations. Issues management provides the linkage between well-developed corporate analytical techniques and public policy issues likely to affect the corporation. It attempts to identify public issues before they become active, develop a corporate position, and then create a strategy to deal with those issues.[4]

Some corporations have expanded and upgraded their Washington offices and made them a more integral part of corporate management. The Atlantic Richfield Company is often cited by the Conference Board as an example of a corporation that has organized itself well to deal with national, state, and local governments. A computer-assisted information system in its Washington office analyzes pending government actions and quickly communicates those analyses to people throughout the organization.[5]

Many corporations are opening Washington offices or joining trade associations headquartered in the area. The Mobil Oil Company has opened a top-level department in Washington to focus on government regulations. An estimated 3,100 national associations, many of them business related, now have headquarters in Washington.[6]

## A CHANGING CORPORATE ENVIRONMENT

Corporate executives' awareness of the impact of government is buttressed by the changing social and ideological underpinnings of the corporation itself. George C. Lodge of the Harvard Business School argues that the traditional U.S. ideology, based on the natural laws formulated by John Locke in the seventeenth century, is giving way.

Lodge sees society moving away from individualism, ideology based on property rights, markets driven by competition and consumer desires, and a limited government role. He detects instead an emerging ideology based on the precedence of political and social issues over property rights, and community needs over individual or consumer desires. This new ideology would encourage active state intervention, and interdependence rather than independence.[7]

Professor Lodge's comments suggest that we are entering an era when the corporate environment will be much more complex, controversial, and demanding. Corporate executives' ability to cope in an environment of heavy government-business interaction is likely to be a new standard for judging their success.

## CONSTITUTIONAL RESTRAINTS ON GOVERNMENT MANAGEMENT

The substantial problems of government management—and those of outsiders in dealing with government—have deep historical roots. When the U.S. Constitution was adopted two hundred years ago, most other governments were corrupt and wasteful, controlled by a few powerful, privileged individuals, and arbitrary in their treatment of the population. Government power is and always has been awesome and easy to abuse. A cursory reading of world history substantiates this unhappy truth, and even today, most governments around the world retain many alarming and negative characteristics. The Constitution was drafted to deliberately limit government power, to help ensure that arbitrary and corrupt activities would be minimized, and to distribute this controlled power more broadly.

Their experience under the English kings and the colonial governors had taught the Founding Fathers a lesson in power politics. The U.S. Constitution was their response. As Jefferson expressed it in the Kentucky Resolutions of 1778:

Free government is founded on jealousy, and not confidence which prescribes limited constitutions to bind down those whom we are obliged to trust with power: that our Constitution has accordingly fixed the limits to which and no further our confidence may go. . . . In questions of power then let no more be heard of confidence in man, but bind him down from mischief by the chain of the Constitution.

Although business and government managers share an interest in good management, management capability, as it is understood in the private sector, is restrained in government by the Constitution. The major goal of the framers of the Constitution was to divide and control power, preventing its concentration in one person or in one small group. They attained their goal; peacetime power has never been concentrated in only a few hands in this country. But the Constitution creates a difficulty, perhaps impossible, management structure for government. Modern management in the private sector has moved toward concentrating power, not dispersing it. If students of contemporary management were to lay the Constitution beside a modern management text, they would find little in common between the two.

The authors of the Constitution were also concerned about the dangers of democratic government, the "tyranny of the majority." They knew that government could not be run by the masses. But the prevailing opinion favored making it impossible for any individual or small group of individuals to run the government alone. These underlying constitutional principles explain in part why business executives have difficulty meshing their management styles with those of government managers.

The Constitution divides power in several ways: between national government and the states, between the two houses of Congress, between Congress and the president, and between all these branches of government and the courts. Creating a modern management system against this backdrop is not easy. The rise of participatory management notwithstanding, nearly all the precepts of modern management call for chief executives who are strong decisionmakers; this requirement runs counter to the philosophy underlying the Constitution and the prohibitions written in it.

For the corporate executive, government is a set of paradoxes. It is opportunity and it is headaches. It is something to be alternately courted and shunned. Little in business-government relations is very clear, with one exception. Government is a major force in the business environment; it has been so for some time and its importance is unlikely to diminish. As concern grows over the U.S. balance of payments, declining productivity, and the competitiveness of the economy in general, the nature of the relationship between business and government will be scrutinized more closely. Other nations—particularly our most successful competitors—organize their business-government relationships differently. The competition will encourage the United States to examine different approaches and perhaps even try a few of them.

## IMPROVING THE EXECUTIVE'S UNDERSTANDING OF GOVERNMENT

The goal of this book is to assist executives of large and small corporations—and those who aspire to executive positions—to become more knowledgeable about government and how it operates. Corporate executives study corporate management, but government management is different. Understanding the differences and learning the paths of government decisionmaking should not only enhance a CEO's corporate skills but also improve the position of that CEO's corporation.

Business and government are the two most powerful institutions in American society today. Each is constrained by a myriad of forces— some legal or constitutional, and others social and political. Yet business and government have come to realize that many of their interests are similar even if the way they operate is quite dissimilar. The topics covered in this book have been selected to cast light on those aspects of government operations and business-government relations that are most important to executives. Subjects discussed include the differences between government and business management; the sources of the love-hate relationship between the two sectors, namely, government regulation and government support of business; characteristics of government managers; and the operation of government decisionmaking structures and how to be effective in them.

We hope that reading this book will improve an executive's ability to manage and to contribute to improving the old but shaky partnership between business and government in the United States.

### NOTES

1. Chandler is quoted in an interesting essay by Bruce L.R. Smith, "The Adversarial Nature of Government-Business Relations in the United States" (Paper for the Donald S. McNaughton Symposium, Syracuse University,

Syracuse, New York, March 1983). See also David Vogel, *National Styles of Regulation: Environmental Policy in Great Britain and the United States* (Ithaca, N.Y.: Cornell University Press, 1986) for an interesting elaboration on this point.

2.  Thomas C. Cochran, *Business in American Life: A History* (New York: McGraw-Hill, 1972), p. 116.

3.  Steiner and Jones are quoted in Rogene A. Buchholz, William D. Evans, and Robert A. Wagley, *Management Response to Public Issues: Concepts and Cases in Strategy Formulation* (Englewood Cliffs, N.J.: Prentice–Hall, 1985), pp. 18, 33.

4.  Rogene A. Buchholz, *Essentials of Public Policy for Management* (Englewood Cliffs, N.J.: Prentice–Hall, 1985),

5.  Phyllis S. McGrath, *Action Plans for Public Affairs* (New York: The Conference Board, 1977). This report also contains suggestions on how other companies might replicate the ARCO program.

6.  Steven V. Roberts, "Trade Associations Are Flocking to Capital as U.S. Widens Its Role," *New York Times*, 4 March 1978. See also *American Society of Association Executives Association Fact Book* (Washington, D.C.: ASAE, 1985).

7.  See George C. Lodge, *The New American Ideology* (New York: Alfred A. Knopf, 1975).

# 2 PUBLIC AND PRIVATE SECTORS
## Differences and Similarities

For corporate executives wishing to improve their relations with government, it is essential to understand the differences between public- and private-sector management. There are differing views on this subject. Arjay Miller, former Ford Motor Company executive and later dean of the Stanford Graduate School of Business, has argued that government is becoming more like business. Governments "have to deal with scarce resources in the public sector—money, land, air, water."[1] Private business has been dealing with limited resources all along. J. Peter Grace, head of the W.R. Grace Company, recently reviewed government management for President Reagan and concluded that government management must become more like business management or government will fail.[2] Years ago the late Wallace Sayre of Columbia University gave the opposite view: that business and public management are alike in every *unimportant* respect.

All these views are partially correct. Business management techniques are increasingly useful to government, but there are substantial differences in the working environments of private and public managers. Thus different applications of management techniques are required. Private executives who think corporate management techniques will solve public policy problems are likely to be disappointed. The public system was designed to accommodate political differences; applying modern management methods is not the primary concern of government.

## THE UNDERLYING DIFFERENCES

Alan K. Campbell, former head of the U.S. Office of Personnel Management, described the differences between public and private management:

> The private manager's major concern is profitability, while in the public sector managers must contend to a greater extent with more ambiguous measures of impact such as social values, the general public interest, accountability to both the law and elected and appointed officials, and the needs of specially targeted groups or individuals. The decision-making process in the public sector, given the demand for openness and the ability of competing groups or individuals to have access to the process, is at least different in degree from what exists in the private sector.[3]

There is a place for business management techniques in government, and there is a need for business executives to work in government from time to time, as many do. The differences in the two environments, however, often produce frustration and even despair. Professor George A. Steiner has noted these feelings:

> I have seen businessmen come to high executive positions in Washington with unsullied reputations for superior managerial efficiency and, after a short time, leave in frustration because the governmental managerial task baffled them. Managing in government is far different from managing in business, aside from the difference in rationality and efficiency. The entire milieu is different. Requirements for managerial success are different. The rules of the game are different.[4]

Steiner does not mean that sound business practices cannot be applied in government. His point is that these practices must be applied in modified ways, though the results may still be unexpected.

Several differences between public and private management are especially apparent to those who have worked in both. But first among them is the difference between one system driven by profits and the other by the give-and-take of politics. In the private sector, most business executives are motivated by the desire to earn a profit for the company. With no profit motive in the public sector, other inducements for increasing efficiency and productivity must be found.

## Operational Differences

W. Michael Blumenthal, secretary of the Treasury under President Carter and CEO of the Unisys, reflected upon some of the challenges a business executive faces coming into government.[5] The difference between appearance and reality is much greater in the public sector. Because profits are the bottom line in business, results usually take precedence over the way business people accomplish them. In government the opposite is often true. How bureaucrats do something may create an image of power that is more important than what they have actually done. If bureaucrats are perceived as powerful, their bargaining positions are enhanced and they are better able to achieve their agency's goals as well as their own.

Blumenthal also cites the relative inability of government managers to change their minds freely. Business executives armed with new facts, better advice, or revised forecasts can alter their decisions and steer businesses or product lines in new directions. When public-sector executives change their minds, often because of new data, they are accused of being weak, indecisive, and inconsistent.

In the private sector, managers can hire people because they are good administrators. Unless they are impeded by collective bargaining agreements, business executives can close plants, reassign personnel, and terminate programs. In the Treasury Department, however, Blumenthal found that most of the managers working for him were either inexperienced political appointees or career civil servants. They were not necessarily chosen for their jobs because they possessed managerial skills; rather, most were hired for their expertise in a specific program area, such as the public debt. Moreover, Blumenthal found it was difficult to hire, fire, reward, or transfer any of his management staff. To drastically change or terminate a program, he would first have to navigate a maze of interest groups, including clients, congressional committees, and even his own employees. Each group had its own reasons for perpetuating the targeted program.

Secretary Blumenthal noticed that private and public employees do not share the same motivations:

> In private industry you have many ways of motivating people. I can say to a young person coming up the latter, as I did, you're doing a hell of a job, and though you're only twenty-seven years old, you've demonstrated that you have the maturity and the ability of a thirty-five-year-old, you have the wis-

dom of a forty-year-old, and I see in you the potential to be the chairman of this company some time, even though you're only twenty-seven, so I'm going to move you around very quickly. I'm going to raise your pay to keep you in the company. . . . And I can set up a system in the company to pick out the bright young people to do that with, and really develop quality in the company.

That's impossible in the government. . . . You have almost no control over selection. Hiring goes off a list. And to go outside that system involves more bureaucratic footwork than it is worth.[6]

There is also the problem of what Blumenthal calls "the inverted pyramid." In the private sector, the work load resembles a pyramid, with top executives working hard but delegating tasks downward to their hand-picked departmental staffs. In the public sector, Blumenthal observes that "government bureaucracy, in terms of work load, is an inverted pyramid. The amount of work varies with how far up you are – the people at the top do most of the work and have most of the pressures and cannot delegate."[7]

Blumenthal sees the top managers in government as hardworking, competent executives who are overloaded, underpaid, and trapped by being unable to right the pyramid and get the management help they need to redistribute the work load.

Roy Ash, who headed the Office of Management and Budget after having been the CEO of Litton Industries, went to the heart of the problem: "Just imagine yourself as chief executive officer where your board is made up of your employees, customers, suppliers and competitors. How would you like to run that business and try to be effective?"[8]

## Legal Limitations

The constitutional, statutory, and traditional limitations imposed on government managers are at the root of the frustration felt by business people when they work in government. Take openness, for example. Public bureaucracies are required to operate openly. They must provide a public record of almost all of their activities for everyone to see. Budgets, job descriptions, salaries, records of revenues and expenditures, and lists of grant and contract awards are considered public information. Legislation is proposed and adopted only after open hearings have been held and both proponents and opponents have been allowed to testify. The transcripts of these hearings are published, as are the voting records of the legislators. Agencies often hold open hearings when a rule is written to implement a program. Public records are also kept of major decisions taken without hearings. The review of NASA's *Challenger* tragedy in January 1986 was a dramatic example of agency decisionmaking being publicly scrutinized in minute detail. Furthermore, judicial review may be invoked if an agency violates established procedures for openness.

The media devotes considerable attention to government activity. The glare of publicity, even on apparently minor matters, is often difficult for the government executive to take, although most view it as a healthy imperative of democratic government.

Public agency decision processes are often criticized for not being open enough or for being open only to the "wrong" people. This criticism is as old as the republic itself. But with the exception of some defense and intelligence agencies, government offices are more open than most business corporations. Corporate deliberations are often conducted in closed meetings. The minutes may be circulated to decisionmakers within the corporation, but not released to the public unless the corporation is under court order.

Another important management difference between the two sectors is that high-level government executives rotate in and out of their positions according to decisions made in voting booths. Management proficiency usually has little influence on electoral success. The Constitution requires periodic elections of top executives—the president, governors, mayors, and many others. The electoral winners are expected to staff their administrations with people who share their policy goals. Over 1,000 top-level appointments are made by a new president, half of them requiring Senate confirmation. In addition, the president will make about 2,500 lower-level appointments. These changes often place public organizations at a great disadvantage compared to private organizations. Many new executives have not worked in government before and need time to learn the laws, rules, court decisions, and cultures of their new organizations. Their middle managers and clients find that the lack of continuity in agency policies and procedures from one presidential appointee to the next causes delay and confusion. Two years is the average length of service in the federal government for these new officials. Such instability and inexperience in the top echelons create major impediments to good management.

Business corporations are generally more orderly in replacing top executives. Rarely do they remove the top echelon all at once, down to and including managers of major operating departments. Even in cases of wholesale change, new top executives are often chosen from within the organization. This tends to reduce the shock waves, ensuring continuity and corporate stability in the eyes of employees, stockholders, and customers.

## Contrasting Functions

Along with constitutional limitations on government, contrasting functions are the primary difference between government and private bureaucracies. Private organizations are created for a specific purpose: to produce a product or deliver a service, at a profit. Many public bureaucracies, on the other hand, are created to represent and serve various constituencies in American society.

Public agencies are under constant pressure to provide satisfactory services to their client groups. Government bureaus represent most major interests in society and many special interests are represented within the larger departments. The Department of Commerce, for example, not only performs the functions normally associated with "commerce" but also encompasses the National Oceanic and Atmospheric Administration (which formerly included the Weather Bureau), the Maritime Administration (with jurisdiction over the Merchant Marine), the National Bureau of Standards, the National Fire Prevention and Control Administration, the Patent and Trademark Offices, and the Economic Development Administration. The secretary of commerce must respond to all the client groups whose interests are represented by Commerce Department agencies. The cabinet secretary does not expect the department agencies representing various interests always to operate in harmony, any more than one expects these interests to interact harmoniously in society at large.

A public bureaucracy is the image of the society that created it. Although cabinet secretaries work for and have been appointed by the same president, there is no reason to expect them to agree on all issues. To be successful, the labor and commerce secretaries must share and represent the views of their constituents. They are likely to agree on issues only to the extent that their respective clients, labor and business, agree in the world outside of government. In government even the most fundamental goals and purposes of one department are likely to be at odds with those of another.

These conflicts between departments in their basic interests and goals are likely to perplex private-sector executives. Internal conflicts are far from uncommon in the private sector. But the authority to deal with internal conflict is more clearly defined and resolution is thus easier to bring about. Corporations can remove executives by kicking them upstairs, moving them out on a "golden parachute," or firing them outright. By contrast, President Reagan found it difficult to fire his secretary of health and human services. He had to locate a vacant ambassadorship before it could be done. Conflict resolution by temporary solutions and fragile alliances is more common in government management than in corporate management.

The Department of Agriculture provides many examples of fragile alliances and temporary solutions. The secretary of agriculture and his staff oversee a bureaucracy that represents many conflicting interests. The department's primary mission is to improve American agricultural production and to represent the interests of all farmers. But the techniques for achieving better production are often hotly debated between large corporate farms and smaller family-run farms. Furthermore, the department is also charged with regulating farm production through its responsibility for meat and food inspection. It runs extensive school lunch and nutritional programs as well as a major welfare program, food stamps. The Farmers Home Administration, another division of the department, is one of the ten largest banking institutions in the United States. Yet nearly one-half of all the employees of the Department of Agriculture work for another division, the U.S. Forest Service.

The interests of the farmer and those of welfare, consumer, and conservation groups often collide. Being secretary of agriculture can be a frustrating task. Issues of agricultural production, regulation, food distribution, and conservation that are argued in society's political arenas are also hotly debated within the department.

To some extent the intense frustration of government executives is a new phenomenon. In the 1950s and 1960s, the Department of Agriculture had only a few client groups representing the diverse interests of the American farmer. While that community often lacked unanimity, the disagreement it engendered within the department was nothing like it is today, when the department serves a vast, multifaceted clientele. Agriculture Department "clients" now include food stamp recipients, school children, timber companies, food processing corporations, and consumers. Decisions at Agriculture can send billion-dollar shock waves through the U.S. economy. This is a substantial change from the relatively quiet, more halcyon days when agriculture production and support for the farm community were the primary departmental focuses.

## DIFFICULTIES OF PUBLIC MANAGEMENT

The government manager is often placed in the awkward position of having to administer laws that are imprecise in scope and intent. Public agencies have their goals and objectives set for them by legislative bodies that create and fund the agencies. The legislation is often vague and ambiguous. Terms like "quality education," "adequate transportation," "decent housing," and "safe streets" are difficult to translate into meaningful operational objectives. In fact, these terms are often used only to ensure passage of the legislation. When conflicting groups in the legislative process cannot agree on specifics, it may be necessary to avoid them, pass the legislation, and leave operational matters until later. Agency executives then have to sort out real objectives from rhetorical ones.

A large portion of the government budget today is devoted to human services programs, which seek to combat some of the nation's major social problems. People living in different regions of the country have various individual and geographically based views of these problems. This means that only the most general statements of program goals will satisfy enough people to ensure program passage and funding. Government management problems are complicated by these generalized mandates to achieve goals that are difficult to measure. In the 1940s, for example, Congress mandated "decent, safe and sanitary housing" for all Americans. Two obvious questions government managers had to answer in the early stages of implementation were What is decent, and, By when?

The Grace Commission, a group of senior business executives organized by President Reagan to study the operations of the federal government, did much useful work toward answering these questions. But the investigators were often frustrated by differences between the private and public sectors. J. Peter Grace, chairman of the group, cogently summed up his frustration with public management:

> As we continued our analysis of government operations, we kept running into a basic obstruction of improving operating efficiency. We found that Congress interferes constantly with the day-to-day management of Federal agencies and departments, contrary to all rules of good management.[9]

He seems to be saying that if only Congress would leave governing to the managers, the system might work. There is little chance of that happening in a democratic system, however, and for good reasons.

The U.S. Postal Service provides many case studies of the frustrations of public management. In many ways the Postal Service is like a typical business organization. Specific operational goals can be set, and the efficiency of the system in attaining those goals can be assessed by standard measurement techniques. One can, for example, determine the time and costs of moving a letter or a package from address A to address B. With that information, it becomes feasible to measure efficiency and, over time, management improvement or degeneration.

But the Postal Service seems less like a business organization and more like a government organization when one examines one social policy it is required to implement, namely, the proposition that all U.S. citizens should receive the same level and quality of government services no matter where they live. This has been interpreted to mean that the Postal Service must provide everyone the same access to a post office whether they live in rural Winterset, Iowa, or in suburban Chevy Chase, Maryland. To implement that policy, the Postal Service has to maintain service in areas where it is not profitable; some argue that it should continue to operate post offices in virtually every crossroads in America.

The postmaster general has a list of a few thousand post offices that do not pay their own way and are not essential to the efficient maintenance of the total system. Using business management techniques, the postmaster general can determine that a facility in Crossroads, U.S.A. moves too little mail and sells too little postage to offset the costs of staffing and maintaining the building. Yet a businesslike decision to close the facility cannot be made, and the office is kept open to fulfill the policy of equal service for all citizens. Furthermore, if the postmaster general decides to close this postal facility, that decision can be appealed to an independent regulatory commission, the Postal Rate Commission (PRC).

The Postal Rate Commission has ruled that the Postal Service may not close rural post offices simply for economic reasons. Pointing to the congressional mandate that other factors be taken into consideration, the PRC has ruled that the effect on the community must be a part of the decision. Post offices provide important community support and communication services beyond the delivery of mail, according to the commission.

The Postal Service is also challenged by the tradition that it support or subsidize certain types of mailings by carrying them at low rates. No amount of sound business management analysis will change this situation. These are matters of social policy, not management. Over the years the government has decided that it should encourage business, nonprofit organizations, charities, and educational institutions through the subsidization of a distribution system for their advertising and publications. The business community, especially advertising and publishing, strongly concurs in this judgment.

Putting the Postal Service on a sound business management basis would be relatively easy if management issues were all that had to be considered. As in most government programs, however, sound management judgments in the Postal Service often give way to the nettlesome and complicated issues of social policy and political feasibility.

The business executive coming into government soon recognizes that there is a point at which business management techniques become ineffective and social policy considerations and politics take over. Imagine a continuum with business management techniques on one end and politics on the other; at different and shifting points along that line, management techniques are subordinated in all government agencies to political and social considerations.

A good example of a government agency once run very much like a business organization is the National Aeronautics and Space Administration (NASA) during the manned-flight space program era. In those days the environment in which NASA operated was nothing like the environment in which most government agencies function or, in fact, like the environment in which NASA operates today.

In the early 1960s the president of the United States gave NASA a clear, one-sentence mission: put a man on the moon by the end of the decade and bring him back safely to earth. There is virtually no way to misinterpret that order. Furthermore, this presidential request became a national quest; few Americans disagreed with the goal. With that kind of national consensus, funding came easily and NASA achieved its goal. In terms of management objectives, the task was easy. NASA deployed complex management systems and engineering techniques as efficiently as a large, well-run corporation would have, and accomplished its mission on time.

Things have changed for NASA. Today it is very much like other government programs in that its mission is less clear and more controversial. After the space shuttle disaster of 1986, the role, functions, and management capabilities of the agency became even more ill defined. NASA now must forcefully compete with other government programs for its share of the national budget; its agenda has been exposed to controversy and the unpredictability of public debate.

## DEFINING OBJECTIVES

Business corporations have an easier time establishing goals and objectives. Fewer social and political issues are involved in developing, producing, and marketing corporate product lines. If a corporation wishes to state its objectives in very precise terms, it has universally agreed-upon language to use. Whether stated in terms of net profits, gross sales, new branch offices, stock prices, or mergers and acquisitions, there is a common understanding by those concerned of what is to be achieved. In contrast, government programs, with their vague or ambiguous objectives, are difficult to evaluate because there are no common standards of measurement. Successful program achievement to one observer is a satisfactory or less than satisfactory performance to another. Corporations use much more quantifiable objectives than "adequate health care" to measure their success. Sales, profits, and production are measurable indicators of goal attainment. Efficiency in operations is easier to attain because promotions, bonuses, and raises can be made dependent upon these quantifiable measures of productivity.

Rewards for public-sector personnel are not based on achievements of high sales or profits. Few quantifiable incentives or objectives are involved in salary determinations, even though the federal government does have a productivity measurement system. Since

1970, twenty-eight government functions have been measured each year. These functions are based on data from 350 agencies representing 66 percent of federal employment. The problem with comparison to private-sector productivity is that the functions measured in the government index are the ones easiest to measure but of marginal significance to total government output. For example, printing and duplication costs are part of the index. The number of claims processed by the Social Security Administration in a given period of time is another. Comparisons with private-sector productivity are generally difficult because of differences in both functions and data bases between government and business.

From 1967 to 1981 federal government productivity increased at the rate of 1.5 percent, while productivity in the private sector increased at a rate of 0.8 percent. In 1980-81 the federal rate jumped to 2.8 percent and the private rate remained the same.[10] In spite of the weaknesses in public-private comparisons, it is noteworthy that the government takes productivity measurements seriously. Also, the direction of the statistical indicators is encouraging, although it is contrary to the perceptions of the public.

Business and government managers perform many of the same tasks, and the demands on each can make their work environments equally unstable. But almost all turbulence in the private sector can ultimately be traced to the challenging competitiveness of the marketplace. Government management, on the other hand, must integrate all of the complex interests, goals, and needs of our pluralistic society.

## NOTES

1. "Big Picture Is Not Just the Profit," *Washington Star*, 17 July 1978.
2. J. Peter Grace, "A Businessman's View of Washington," *The Bureaucrat* 13, no. 2 (1984): 14-17.
3. Letter from Alan K. Campbell, chairman of the U.S. Civil Service Commission, to John S. Day, president of the American Assembly of Collegiate Schools of Business, 28 September 1977. Campbell became director of the Office of Personnel Management when the Civil Service Commission was abolished in January 1979.
4. George A. Steiner, *Business and Society*, 2d ed. (New York: Random House, 1975), p. 384.

5.   "Candid Reflections of a Businessman in Washington," *Fortune*, 29 January 1979, pp. 36–49.

6.   Ibid., p. 40.

7.   Ibid.

8.   Gordon Chase, "Managing Compared," *New York Times*, 14 March 1978. Many of the arguments comparing public and private management are summarized in a comprehensive book of readings: James L. Perry and Kenneth L. Kraemer, eds., *Public Management: Public and Private Perspectives* (Palo Alto, Calif.: Mayfield, 1983).

9.   President's Private Sector Survey on Cost Control, *War on Waste* (New York: Macmillan, 1984), 19. This is a commercially published version of the two summary volumes of the Grace Commission report. The forty-seven volumes produced by the survey were not published commercially.

10.  Jerome Mark, "Measuring Productivity in Government: Federal, State and Local," *Public Productivity Review* 5 (1981): 21–44. For an interesting analysis of this data, see Howard Rosen, *Servants of the People: The Uncertain Future of the Federal Civil Service* (Salt Lake City: Olympus, 1985), ch. 7. See also Donald M. Fisk, "Productivity Trends in the Federal Government," *Monthly Labor Review* 108 (1985): 3–9.

# 3 REGULATIONS AND RESPONSES

Government rules and regulations have irritated the business community for decades. The very words *rules and regulations* make business executives uneasy and resentful, and understandably so. No one likes being regulated; moreover, regulation runs counter to the free enterprise philosophy. Yet the business system cannot work without some government rules and regulations to organize and monitor the marketplace.

Historically, business has cooperated with government in formulating rules and regulations. The regulatory system accommodated the business community, and business has learned to live with government's requirements. This picture began to change about twenty-five years ago, however, and today the business community confronts rules and regulations markedly different in type and quantity from those of the past.

Previously, most government regulations were directed at organizing the marketplace and protecting the business environment. Licensing procedures, antimonopolistic efforts, incorporation procedures, and certain financial reporting requirements were the common forms of government intervention. Regulations were more helpful than not. They made it possible for businesses to operate competitively. Without these regulations it would have been difficult and perhaps impossible to create the large commercial and industrial systems that exist in this country today.

In the 1960s and 1970s government became a more active regulator, focusing on the internal activities of business: safety and health in the workplace and equal opportunity for all workers regardless of race, sex, or age. Government also became concerned with the impact of business activities on the physical environment: air, water, land, and endangered species.

These issues are substantially different from the issues underlying past regulation. They have less to do with the orderly operation of enterprise than with the impact of enterprise on society, individuals, and the quality of life in general.

## TWO CLASSES OF GOVERNMENT REGULATION

The shift in the nature of regulation is so pronounced that government regulations now fall into two distinct classes: Regulation I, which is primarily economic, and Regulation II, covering social and environmental concerns.

Regulation I, the older vintage, creates the necessary institutions and ground rules for a competitive environment. Money supply management, enforcement of private contracts, protection of private property, patent and copyright protection, and guarantees to consumers of pure food and drugs are examples of this type. The purpose of these regulations is to encourage competitive forces in the economy, not to supplant them.

Regulation I, comprising the bulk of all regulation, is generally supported by business and, in fact, is usually initiated by groups in the business community. These regulations are slow to be reformed because of the difficulty in garnering public or business support to bring about changes. Although some segment of the business community might desire changes in Regulation I, there are substantial obstacles to achieving consensus for significant change. Also, these regulations have been used to limit entry into certain markets, airline and trucking regulation, for example. Those who are regulated in these markets benefit substantially from regulation and do not want to see it removed.

Regulation II, primarily social and environmental in nature, is a phenomenon of the last thirty years. It grew out of broad-based political movements labeled "environmentalism," "civil rights," "consumerism," and "social activism." Though small in volume compared to Regulation I, this fast-growing regulatory area gives corporations the most difficulty.

This type of regulation attempts to define what goods should or should not be produced. It spells out product specifications and procedures in industrial processes to increase industrial safety, for example. This kind of regulation also defines modes of environmentally acceptable production, types of employees who should be hired, acceptable working conditions, pay equity, retirement systems, and similar issues.

Regulation II is directed more at social than economic policy. New and large groups, such as Common Cause, women's organizations, and a variety of consumer groups, are active in political processes to bring about social changes by requiring business to operate differently.

> The real purpose of government regulation is not to correct the deficiencies of markets but to transcend markets altogether—which is to say, government regulation is not economic policy but social policy. It is an effort to advance a conception of the public interest apart from, and often opposed to, the outcomes of the marketplace and, indeed, the entire idea of a market economy.[1]

Most of the newer regulations apply to the nonprofit sector as well as to business. Universities, churches, state and local governments, and the federal government must meet environmental, equal employment opportunity, and other standards just as their counterparts in the private sector must.

The growth of this type of regulation has fostered a new concern in business about its relationship with government. It has led to the creation or expansion of corporate offices of legislative affairs. In response to Regulation II, many corporations have opened Washington offices and enlisted the support of Washington law firms or lobbying organizations. A major business lobby, the Business Roundtable, has been formed and the National Association of Manufacturers has moved its offices from Chicago to Washington.

### From Economic to Social Regulation

Before the advent of Regulation II, business had grown accustomed to economic regulation and often learned to profit by it. Regulation was the framework that assured the supply, at reasonable terms and prices, of the goods and services necessary for economic growth. In fields such as banking and securities, energy, communications, and transportation, regulation permitted development while reducing the likelihood of systemwide collapses. During the period of expansion into the West, business was inclined to support big, centralized government and its regulatory programs for the stability they provided, which was necessary for economic growth.

In the 1960s the picture changed as a number of noneconomic groups gained sufficient political strength to begin using regulatory agencies to achieve their goals. Congress responded by focusing on social areas; there were few new initiatives in the traditional economic and industrial areas. A listing of major regulatory programs in the order they were established shows this shift in emphasis (see Table 3-1). The shift is from the regulation of relations among sellers, competitors, and customers—begun seriously in 1887 when the Interstate Commerce Commission was formed to regulate the railroads— to the regulation of societal relations, focusing on issues such as the health of the work force and the quality of the environment.

One may argue that by the 1960s the nation had a lot of catching up to do in the social and environmental areas. That might well be true. What is undeniable, however, is that the regulatory process to which business had gradually grown accustomed over the course of nearly 100 years, was suddenly being asked to solve problems far different from those it had been designed to solve.

Economic regulation generally had a well-defined, narrow focus. Regulatory agencies were mandated to address questions of which business structures were permissible and which were not, what accounting and financial disclosures were allowed or required, what advertising might claim and what it might not, and the purity and safety of what might be produced. Social regulation, on the other hand, focuses less on the formal means and output of production and more on the side effects of production, or "externalities" in economic parlance.

The impact of these new regulations on corporate executives was substantial, even traumatic. For individuals trained and experienced in finance, marketing, corporate planning, and business management, having to be concerned with social issues was extraordinary, uninteresting, disruptive, and intrusive.

Furthermore, the procedures that had been established to handle economic regulation do not always work well with the newer social

**Table 3-1.**  Economic and Social Regulation: Major Regulatory Programs by Year of Birth, 1863 to Date.

| Date | Economic and Industrial Regulation (Agency Responsible) | Social Regulation (Agency Responsible) |
|---|---|---|
| 1863 | Chartering and supervision of national banks (Comptroller of the Currency, Department of the Treasury) | |
| 1887 | Railroad regulation (Interstate Commerce Commission) | |
| 1906 | | Food and drug production regulation (Food and Drug Administration, Department of Health and Human Services) |
| 1913 | Supervision of Federal Reserve banks and members banks (Federal Reserve System) | |
| 1914 | Preventing restraints of trade, unfair competition, and false labeling and advertising (Federal Trade Commission) | |
| 1916 | Regulation of offshore waterborne commerce (Federal Maritime Commission) | |
| 1916 | Regulation of import trade (U.S. International Trade Commission) | |
| 1920 | Licensing hydroelectric projects on navigable waters (Federal Energy Regulatory Commission) | |
| 1922 | Regulating commodity futures trading (Commodity Futures Trading Commission | |
| 1932 | Supervision and insurance of savings and loan institutions (Federal Home Loan Bank Board) | |
| 1933 | Supervision of nonmember state banks; deposit insurance (Federal Deposit Insurance Corporation) | |
| 1933 | Preventing of fraud in securities insurance (Securities and Exchange Commission) | |
| 1934 | Radio/TV broadcast licensing (Federal Communications Commission) | |
| 1934 | Regulation of security exchanges (Securities and Exchange Commission) | |

**Table 3-1.** continued

| Date | Economic and Industrial Regulation (Agency Responsible) | Social Regulation (Agency Responsible) |
|------|---------------------------------------------------------|----------------------------------------|
| 1935 | Restructuring and regulation of public utility holding companies (Securities and Exchange Commission) | |
| 1935 | Regulation of interstate wholesale electric traffic (Federal Energy Regulation Commission) | |
| 1935 | | Regulation of collective bargaining (National Labor Relations Board) |
| 1935 | Regulation of motor carriers (Interstate Commerce Commission) | |
| 1938 | Regulation of civil commercial aviation (Civil Aeronautics Board) | |
| 1938 | Regulation of interstate natural gas traffic (Federal Energy Regulatory Commission) | |
| 1946 | Regulation of civilian use of atomic energy (Nuclear Regulatory Commission) | |
| 1948 | | Certification of aircraft types and aircrew (Federal Aviation Administration) |
| 1962 | | Air quality regulation (Environmental Protection Agency) |
| 1963 | | Equal Pay Act (Equal Employment Opportunity Commission) |
| 1964 | | Prevention of discrimination in employment (Equal Employment Opportunity Commission) |
| 1965 | | Water quality regulation (Environmental Protection Agency) |
| 1966 | | Safety regulation of motor carriers (Federal Highway Administration) |
| 1966 | | Safety regulation of railroads (Federal Railroad Administration) |
| 1966 | | Safety and efficiency of motor vehicles (Federal Highway Traffic Safety Administration) |

Table 3-1.  continued

| Date | Economic and Industrial Regulation (Agency Responsible) | Social Regulation (Agency Responsible) |
|---|---|---|
| 1967 | | Preventing age discrimination in employment (Equal Employment Opportunity Commission) |
| 1968 | | Full disclosure of credit terms ("Truth in Lending") (Federal Reserve System and Federal Trade Commission) |
| 1968 | | Regulating interstate firearms trade (Bureau of Alcohol, Tobacco, and Firearms, Treasury Department) |
| 1970 | Promoting uniformity of accounting among government contractors (Cost Accounting Standards Board) | |
| 1970 | | Regulating occupational safety and health performance (Occupational Safety and Health Administration, Labor Department) |
| 1970 | Supervising Federal credit unions (National Credit Union Administration) | |
| 1970 | Regulating postal rates and classifications (Postal Rate Commission) | |
| 1970 | | Securing of environmental impact review of federal projects (Environmental Protection Agency) |
| 1972 | | Regulating safety of consumer products (Consumer Product Safety Commission) |
| 1972 | | Control of noise pollution (Environmental Protection Agency) |
| 1973 | | Regulating lawful trade in narcotic drugs (Drug Enforcement Administration, Justice Department) |
| 1973 | Oil pricing, allocation, and import regulation (Economic Regulatory Administration, Energy Department) | |
| 1973 | | Regulation of mine safety (Mine Safety and Health Administration) |

**Table 3–1.**  continued

| Date | Economic and Industrial Regulation (Agency Responsible) | Social Regulation (Agency Responsible) |
|---|---|---|
| 1973 | | Employment of handicapped persons (Employment Standards Administration, Department of Labor) |
| 1974 | | Supervision of pension plans (Pension Benefit Guaranty Corporation) |
| 1975 | | Transportation accident investigation; regulation of accident reporting (National Transportation Safety Board) |
| 1975 | | Mortgage disclosure eliminating "redlining" (Federal Deposit Insurance Corporation) |
| 1975 | | Standards for written warranties (Federal Trade Commission) |
| 1976 | | Toxic substance control (Environmental Protection Agency) |
| 1976 | | Equal credit opportunity to eliminate sex discrimination in lending (Federal Deposit Insurance Corporation) |
| 1977 | | Water quality standards (Environmental Protection Agency) |
| 1978 | | Energy conservation standards for utilities (Federal Energy Regulatory Commission) |
| 1978 | Regulation of foreign banks operating in U.S. (Federal Deposit Insurance Corporation) | |
| 1980 | | Toxic waste cleanup; "Superfund" (Environmental Protection Agency) |
| 1984 | | Greater equity in pension plans for workers and spouses (Pension Benefit Guaranty Corporation) |
| | | Stiffened penalties for "insider trading" (Securities and Exchange Commission) |
| 1985 | | Prohibit receipt of stolen property from ,banks and bribing bank personnel (Federal Deposit Insurance Corporation) |

Source:  A. Lee Fritschler, *The Changing Face of Government Regulations* (New York: Maxwell Graduate School Publication, Syracuse University, 1980), pp. 12–13. (Updated by the authors.)

regulations. It is often impossible to foresee the impact of a social regulation on costs, benefits, or individuals. Setting long-distance phone rates is quite a different matter from setting rules and quotas for the hiring of women and minorities or setting limitations on the release of pollutants into the environment. Economic regulations most directly affect those who are being regulated. Social regulations can affect large groups in society whether or not they participate in the regulation procedure.

## Costs and Effects of Regulation

The slowdown in national economic growth that began in the mid–1970s raised serious questions about the effect of regulation on the economy. No one attributes the nation's macroeconomic problems entirely to government regulations; there are dozens of other factors, ranging from insufficient support of education to disincentives to invest. Some of these economic problems, however, can be attributed to a reduction in managerial productivity. Corporate managers may have been diverted from efficient management of the enterprise to less relevant, less productive external factors. Edward F. Denison of The Brookings Institution claims:

> Profitability of a business is now affected far more than it was before the 1970s by its responses to rapid changes in government regulations and tax codes. Failure to learn of and conform to regulations can have serious legal consequences, including criminal penalties. Failure to find the cheapest way to conform can be expensive. Failure to learn of proposals for new laws or regulations and to participate in hearings and to use other channels to help shape their final form can bring permanently higher costs or loss of markets, as can failure to foresee changes in laws and regulations and to take timely action in advance to minimize losses or maximize gains from the changes. Not only are laws and regulations actually proposed or made effective pertinent; one must anticipate possible future proposals.[2]

It is not surprising that the growth of social and environmental regulation, together with a decline in economic growth, led to demands for deregulation and regulatory reform.

The cost of government regulation and its impact on inflation has become an economic and political issue in the United States. Measuring the cost of regulation is, of course, very difficult. Measuring the benefits of regulation is even more difficult. And determining the impact of these costs and benefits on the economy is more difficult still.

Looking only at the budgeted costs of administering regulatory programs, one notices a wide range of estimates of the federal government's expenditures on regulatory programs. Total outlays of the thirteen major regulatory agencies in FY 1987 are estimated to be over $6 billion.[3] Even with deregulation these figures have grown from about $3 billion in 1976 and may continue to grow.[4] These figures would have to be multiplied by a large factor to include the expenditures of other federal agencies with regulatory responsibilities, like the Department of Agriculture, or expenditures on regulatory programs of state and local governments. Even so, these administrative costs are only a part of the story.

The real burden of regulation comes in the increased costs of manufacturing, sales, and management in the private sector. Professor Murray Weidenbaum of Washington University has compiled a list of these extra costs imposed by regulatory programs. His list includes:

1.  Higher production costs due to regulation by the Consumer Products Safety Commission, Environmental Protection Agency, Occupational Safety and Health Administration, and other federal agencies

2.  Higher personnel costs resulting from federally mandated fringe benefits such as social security, unemployment insurance, and workers' compensation

3.  Higher interest rates as financial markets react to increased demand generated by various federal loan guarantee programs

4.  Higher government procurement costs because of federal contracting regulations that require suppliers to hire on a nondiscriminatory basis, provide safe working conditions, pay prevailing wages, and give preference to U.S. products in their purchases[5]

## Deregulation Efforts and Successes

Building upon a latent base of public support for reducing both the size of government and its impact on society, deregulation activities have made substantial progress over the last several years. Presidents

Ford, Carter, and Reagan have made major changes in the regulatory system. Shortly after assuming office, President Ford created a high-level staff group in the White House that reviewed the regulatory programs of several federal agencies. The results of their studies were included in Ford's first economic report (1976). President Ford subsequently proposed legislation to deregulate the airline, trucking, and railroad industries. Only the railroad proposal, however, reached the point of serious congressional consideration during his administration.

The Carter years saw deregulation of the airline, trucking, railroad, and banking industries and oil and natural gas pricing. A combination of administrative actions, Federal Communications Commission orders, and court decisions eventually led to divestiture of AT&T and some deregulation in the telecommunications industry. See Table 3–2 for a list of major deregulation initiatives from 1971 to the present.

President Carter moved to improve the management of the remaining regulatory programs. In March 1978 he signed Executive Order No. 12044, which encouraged agencies to (1) devote more attention to planning the regulatory process; (2) facilitate greater public participation in that process; (3) analyze the cost effectiveness of a proposed rule—selecting the least costly alternative to achieve a given objective; (4) reduce the burden of regulation upon small businesses; (5) review regulations regularly and prepare analyses of rules with major economic consequences; (6) establish agency head accountability; (7) set expiration dates so that obsolete rules would not remain on the books; (8) reduce paperwork and write rules in plain English; and (9) develop an improved state and local coordination process.

In October 1978 President Carter also established the Regulatory Council, composed of the heads of thirty-six executive departments and independent regulatory agencies. The council served as the coordinating agency for regulatory reform at the national level. Twice yearly the council published the *Calendar of Federal Regulations*, which encouraged public participation in rulemaking. The *Calendar*, which contained listings of proposed rules having an economic impact of $100 million or more, served as an early warning system for both the regulators and the regulated. The listings were designed to minimize agency duplication and overlap and are still published, although in a different format.

President Reagan has continued the regulatory reform efforts of his predecessors and directed those efforts along new paths. A new

Table 3-2.  Selected Major Deregulatory Actions, 1970-85.

| | |
|---|---|
| 1971 | Federal Communications Commission: Specialized common carrier decision |
| 1972 | Federal Communications Commission: Domestic satellite open skies policy |
| 1975 | Securities and Exchange Commission: Abolition of fixed brokerage fees |
| | Circuit Court of Appeals for the District of Columbia: |
| | *Continental Airlines v. CAB* held the Federal Aviation Act required the Civil Aeronautics Board to foster competition |
| 1976 | Railroad Revitalization and Reform Act |
| 1977 | Air Cargo Deregulation Act |
| | Circuit Court of Appeals for the District of Columbia: |
| | *MCI Telecommunications Corp. v. FCC* upheld a challenge to AT&T's monopoly in public interstate long-distance telephone service |
| 1978 | Airline Deregulation Act: Deregulation of fares and routes |
| | Natural Gas Policy Act: Deregulation of prices |
| | Occupational Safety and Health Administration: Standards revocation |
| | Public Utilities Regulatory Policy Act |
| | Environmental Protection Administration: Emissions trading policy |
| | Executive Order No. 12044: Requirement for regulatory impact statements |
| 1979 | Federal Communications Commission: Deregulation of satellite-earth stations |
| 1980 | Motor Carrier Reform Act |
| | Household Goods Transportation Act |
| | Staggers Rail Act |
| | Securities and Exchange Commission: Exempted small business from securities laws registration requirements |
| | Depository Institutions Deregulation and Monetary Control Act |
| | International Air Transportation Competition Act |
| | Federal Communications Commission: Deregulation of customer premises equipment and enhanced services |
| 1981 | Executive Order No. 12287: Decontrol of crude oil and refined petroleum products |
| | Federal Reserve Board: Truth in lending |
| | Federal Communications Commission: Deregulation of radio broadcast content |
| | Executive Order No. 12291: Expanded Office of Management and Budget authority in regulatory field, and implemented regulatory cost-benefit analysis |
| | Product Safety Amendments: Increased reliance on voluntary standards |

**Table 3–2.** continued

| | |
|---|---|
| 1982 | Bus Regulatory Reform Act |
| | Garn-St Germain Depository Institution Act: Expanded Activities of savings institutions |
| | District Court for the District of Columbia: Modified Final Judgment in *U.S. v. AT&T* |
| 1984 | AT&T divestiture implemented |
| | Cable Deregulation Act |
| | Civil Aeronautics Board Senset Act |
| | Food and Drug Administration: Expedited approval of generic versions of "pioneer" drugs |
| 1985 | Executive Order No. 12498: Required agencies to submit proposed regulations to Office of Management and Budget early in the formulation process |

Source: Roger G. Noll and Bruce M. Owen, *The Political Economy of Deregulation: Interest Groups in the Regulatory Process* (Washington, D.C.: American Enterprise Institute, 1983), p. 4; updated with the addition of various statutes and court decisions.

term, "regulatory relief," was coined. The president and his staff argued that many groups in society, but business in particular, were overburdened with regulations. The burdens included not only too much government interference in markets, but too much report writing, too many forms, and too much necessary attention paid to the regulators in Washington. The president said he wanted the government "off the backs" of the American people.

The Reagan program has extended well beyond the areas in which his predecessors initiated economic deregulation. Certain industries, such as the auto industry, were targeted for economic relief from the burdens of overregulation. The Reagan Administration has also attempted to reduce the impact of environmental and social regulations, pay greater attention to cost-benefit analysis, and strengthen the Office of Management and Budget to better control (or regulate) the regulatory agencies.[6]

By 1983 the Reagan Administration's efforts to decrease the number of new regulations and to extend regulatory relief had slowed down. A major scandal in the Environmental Protection Agency marked the turning point in the president's program. Eventually, the EPA head resigned and one of her deputies was convicted of favoritism toward a corporation involved in the toxic waste program. Dissatisfaction in Congress with various parts of that program led to intensive oversight hearings. Public interest in environmental protection also began to revive. Several court decisions at this time left some existing regulations in place.

In the second Reagan term the regulatory reform and relief program moved from political and legislative arenas to a focus on management improvement. In the summer of 1985 the Reagan administration issued an analysis of the regulatory activities of seventeen agencies, including each agency head's projection of agency regulatory goals for the coming year. The results of this important new procedure for reassessing agency goals are now presented by the president each year in his federal budget proposals.[7]

The Reagan program has succeeded in drawing attention to significant problems in regulation, particularly in the social and environmental areas. The budgets of most regulatory agencies have been reduced, the result being less aggressive regulatory activity. Many regulatory programs have lost steam, and the political issue of regulation has faded for the first time in nearly a decade. Political concerns have shifted to the federal budget, the deficit, and trade matters. Regulatory reform and relief have been moved off center stage and back into the wings; further reform efforts will be handled by presidential and agency staff as a part of the management and planning process.[8]

## BUSINESS SUPPORT FOR REGULATION I

Business executives are understandably ambivalent toward certain regulations. A large portion of Regulation I, however, is generated by private interests. That is, much of it was made law because of the lobbying success of particular businesses or industries striving to improve their positions in the marketplace, which they also hoped to make more stable.

For many decades students of government have criticized regulatory agencies for responding only to the needs of business. This criticism is an exaggeration and an oversimplification. Some agencies were very responsive to business, others were not. The response of some agencies to business interests varied with changes in the public mood and changes in administrations. Over time, however, business played a very strong hand in most agencies, sometimes prevailing over other players.

Business had the stronger hand only because most of those involved in regulatory decisionmaking were business representatives. Representatives of consumers and the general public were poorly organized and relatively inactive. Consequently, there are many regulations that make it difficult for new businesses to enter the market, as well as regulations giving one type of product a competitive edge over another. Until twenty years ago this type of regulation made up almost the whole regulatory arsenal of at least one agency, the Federal Trade Commission (FTC).

When transistor radios first became popular they began to appear on the shelves of discount houses and drugstores at very low prices. They were often advertised as having twelve or fifteen transistors and were being sold for under $10. The established radio manufacturers knew that it was impossible to produce a twelve- or fifteen-transistor radio and sell it for $10 or less. They investigated the claim and discovered that while the new radios had the advertised number of transistors, only two or three transistors were part of the radio circuit. The rest were dummies wired to the chassis.

The radio manufacturers asked the FTC for a hearing and were granted it. They made their case and then asked the commission to require radio advertisements to claim only the number of transistors operating in the radio circuit. It was a very short hearing. The commissioners saw the reasonableness of the manufacturers' request and wrote the regulation. Another rule was thus enacted, creating more red tape and new enforcement mechanisms. Ironically, the enforcement requirements of regulation that businesses object to—such as the expense and added work of reporting—were generated by this decision. Yet the commission had moved at the request of an industry for help with its problem in the marketplace.

A classic example of industry-government cooperation is the development of regulation in the pure foods area. The early manufacturers of canned and packaged foods knew that the industry could not grow unless the public had confidence in their new products. So the industry worked with government to set high safety and purity standards that all food packagers had to meet. Without these standards, unscrupulous suppliers could have soured the marketplace, damaging the prospects of success for reputable companies. This business-government collaboration has worked well.

The Flammable Fabrics Act of 1967 is another regulation gener-ated by private interests. In congressional hearings arguments were presented for each side by different businesses in the clothing indus-try: the chemical fiber manufacturers supported the act, while the natural fiber manufacturers opposed it. The former group, makers of fire-retardant products, won the debate. The public also benefited, of course, but there was almost no public participation in the legis-lative process, which was primarily a debate between industrial giants. Once again a new regulation was promulgated, with all the accompanying paperwork and enforcement activity.

The private sector uses government regulation to resolve conflicts in the business community to keep the marketplace viable and to bring about adjustments that, for better or worse, the marketplace could not make on its own.

## BUSINESS PROBLEMS WITH REGULATION II

The politics of Regulation II are different from the politics of Regu-lation I. Social, environmental, and consumers' groups initiated Regulation II, with the support of broad coalitions that do not have direct economic stakes in the decisions of government. Phrases like "quality of life" and "equal opportunity" replaced "marketplace," "profits," and similar terms in the language of regulation.

Regulation II is a difficult area for business, partly because these regulations often reflect social policy controversies. For example, regulations imposed on the nuclear energy industry are viewed by that industry as restraints on economic growth and therefore as inimical to business. On the other hand, environmentalists argue that since the dangers of nuclear energy production are so great and potentially harmful to both people and the environment, regulation must not only continue but be strengthened.

Oil company exploration processes are also subject to numerous government regulations designed to protect the environment. Oil companies view the regulations as too stringent and costly, while environmental groups see them as reasonable protections. Equal em-ployment regulations can be difficult and costly for small businesses and most nonprofit organizations; civil rights and women's groups feel that they are essential to social progress. With Regulation II, one can see some of the major social issues of our time being fought out. Reasonable debate is healthy for a dynamic, democratic society but not especially helpful to the improvement of business-government relations.

## THE COMPLICATED POLITICS OF DEREGULATION

The change in government regulation from an economic to a social and environmental focus has fostered a corresponding change in how businesses lobby in Washington. For years the U.S. Chamber of Commerce and the National Association of Manufacturers were the major voices in Washington for the business community. Although they took strong positions on many issues, these organizations found it difficult to formulate a position on government regulation because of the lack of consensus among their members. It was nearly impossible to reach more than 20 or 30 percent agreement among member businesses on any economic regulation issue. Regulations opposed by one business or industry were almost always beneficial to others. Because most major corporations belong to these two groups (as do hundreds of smaller companies), each found itself taking both sides of most regulatory issues. It is impossible to lobby effectively while so divided.

For example, airline deregulation posed problems for the Chamber of Commerce. The trunk carriers opposed deregulation, but the feeder airlines favored deregulation, as did many of the businesses in the smaller cities they serviced. The chamber was frozen into silence by these competing interests. This dilemma reflects the larger conflict within the business community on the issue of government regulation and typifies the politics of deregulation. The large, well-established corporations saw economic deregulation as a threat to their superior market positions. The national truck lines fought interstate deregulation. AT&T vigorously opposed deregulation that allowed competition in long-distance telecommunications. The large banks feared the competition from new kinds of financial institutions offering traditional financial services, and therefore did not support the deregulation proposals that ultimately changed their industry.

Nevertheless, a substantial amount of economic deregulation occurred in the late 1970s and early 1980s. The politics of deregulation were surprisingly unconventional. There were no large-scale coalitions lobbying for deregulation, and consumers seemed uninterested in the idea. The economists and others who favored deregulation were a lonely and often dispirited collection of people. Certain leaders encouraged the deregulation movement, including Presidents Ford, Carter, and Reagan, some members of Congress, and the heads of several independent regulatory commissions. These leaders pushed for reform, and the results were substantial.

Several industries were restructured, and changes were also made in pricing, service delivery, and products. Many of the results were unpredictable, like the eventual support for deregulation by some industry leaders who had been long opposed to it. But the most surprising outcome is the great extent to which the government has unleashed marketplace forces upon industries that were once tightly controlled by regulation.[9]

Success in economic deregulation did not carry over to social and environmental regulation. These regulations, however, have changed the way business lobbies in Washington.

The Business Roundtable, founded in 1972, is a business lobby composed of the CEOs of more than 200 of the nation's largest corporations. It has a small Washington staff, but the members themselves decide on agendas and do much of the representational work, using their own corporate staffs for support. Although the Roundtable examines economic issues, such as taxation and wage and price controls, it is also concerned with the impact of social and environmental regulations on U.S. business. The emergence of these new regulations enabled the major corporations to unite their positions on the corresponding issues. Regulation II has had an industrywide impact and it is now easier for the business community to present government with a united front.

Problems remain, however, in developing industrywide positions. Regulation II involves complex and controversial policy issues with no clear or final solutions. H.L. Mencken once said that all major social problems have easy solutions that are "neat, plausible and wrong." As the Roundtable works on the issues involved in Regulation II, it is encountering the same difficulties experienced by Congress, various administrations, and the general public. Its members are struggling to reach agreement.

Standing in the way of a truly united business coalition is the fact that there are few government regulations, even in Regulation II, that do not benefit at least some businesses. For example, many corporations find air pollution control requirements burdensome, but new corporations are joining established ones like Boeing and Combustion Engineering to develop new lines of air pollution control equipment. Between 1972 and 1976 the pollution control industry grew at an annual rate of 20 percent, compared with a 9 percent annual growth rate for all manufacturing companies.[10]

This is not the only example. Higher mileage standards on automobiles have led to the creation of new technology and new markets for more sophisticated equipment. Air bag devices in automobiles are opposed by the auto industry and much of the public, but for some time now the insurance industry has supported a regulation requiring them. It would be hard to find a regulation that does not have some important industrial backers. The longer a regulation is on the books, the more business support it gains.

Although there are many areas of government where business has good reason to exert its influence, regulation is probably the key area where business and government meet head on. Over time it is the area of greatest contention. Yet the impact of regulation on business is not always negative. In fact, it is widely accepted that commerce could not go forward and the economy could not keep growing without some government supervision of the marketplace. Business and government have a love-hate relationship, and nothing illustrates it better than the give-and-take of government's regulatory control over business.

## NOTES

1.  Paul H. Weaver, "Regulation, Social Policy and Class Conflict," *The Public Interest*.50 (1978): 45.
2.  Edward F. Denison, *Trends in American Economic Growth, 1929–1982* (Washington, D.C.: The Brookings Institution, 1985), pp. 44–45.
3.  Office of Management and Budget, *Budget of the United States Fiscal Year 1987* (Washington, D.C.: U.S. Government Printing Office, 1986). See figures for major regulatory agencies.
4.  Robert E. Litan and William D. Nordhaus, *Reforming Federal Regulation* (New Haven: Yale University Press, 1983), pp. 127–31.
5.  Murray L. Weidenbaum, *Government-Mandated Price Increases: A Neglected Aspect of Inflation* (Washington, D.C.: American Enterprise Institute for Public Policy Research, 1975), chs. 5–8.

6.  See two books by George C. Eads and Michael Fix, eds.: *The Reagan Regulatory Strategy: An Assessment* (Washington, D.C.: Urban Institute Press, 1984) and *Relief or Reform? Reagan's Regulatory Dilemma* (Washington, D.C.: Urban Institute Press, 1984). See also Executive Order No. 12291, 46 Fed. Reg. 13193 (1981).

7.  Office of Management and Budget, *Regulatory Program of the United States Government, April 1, 1985–March 31, 1986* (Washington, D.C.: U.S. Government Printing Office, 1985).

8.  For more information on the Reagan regulatory efforts, see Kenneth J. Meier, *Regulation: Politics, Bureaucracy, and Economics* (New York: St. Martin's Press, 1985); Susan J. and Martin Tolchin, *Dismantling America: The Rush to Deregulate* (New York: Oxford University Press, 1983); and Michael Pertschuk, *Revolt Against Regulation: The Rise and Pause of the Consumer Movement* (Berkeley: University of California Press, 1982).

9.  For an interesting analysis of the politics of deregulation in the airline, trucking, and telecommunications industries, see Martha Derthick and Paul J. Quirk, *The Politics of Deregulation* (Washington, D.C.: The Brookings Institution, 1985).

10. "Pollution Control Business Grows," *Washington Star*, 29 November 1978; see also Hal Hoover's series on "Environmental Controls in Industry," *Washington Post*, especially 15 October 1978.

# 4 THE OTHER SIDE OF THE COIN
## Business-Government Cooperation

Most people believe that business and government are fierce adversaries. There is indeed a long history of sometimes angry conflict between them and, of course, these encounters attract attention. Surprisingly, however, the adversarial nature of business-government relations is neither as common nor as pervasive as popular wisdom would have it.

Over the decades the relationship between these supposed adversaries has been more often characterized by a spirit of partnership and cooperation. It is not unusual for political rhetoric to be out of touch with reality– but in this case the rhetoric is remarkably distant from the reality.

In the past it may not have mattered that most people misperceived business-government interaction. With our nation losing its dominant position in many world markets, however, it is important that we understand better how government has supported business all along, and what it might do to further encourage business in the future. When the United States was the primary manufacturing nation in the world, a position it enjoyed for many years, little thought was given to global competition. The world wanted what we produced, and our exports of both manufactured and agricultural goods were equally strong.

Today competition from abroad is intense, particularly in the area of manufactured goods. Questions about U.S. competitiveness are being raised in many quarters. The public heard the issue debated in the 1984 presidential campaigns. It surfaced then as a campaign issue, but disappeared for a while as the economy began to improve. Predicting the life cycle of a political issue is risky, but there is not much risk in predicting that the competitiveness issue will continue to be a major public concern.

The issue most commonly arises in discussions of our nation's industrial policy. Do we already have an industrial policy or policies? Do we need to develop one overall policy? Would such an industrial policy lead to a centralized bureaucratic mechanism that controls investment and picks industrial winners and losers? Or would it have the less centralized purpose of simply better coordinating existing government programs?

## THE ROOTS OF GOVERNMENT SUPPORT

To make more sense out of this controversial and complicated subject, it helps to look at what role government has played and is currently playing in industrial development and growth. The history of government activity on behalf of business is older than the Constitution itself.

Students of American history might wonder why there is so much controversy today over the question of government involvement in promoting business and industry. Reporting to Congress in 1791, Alexander Hamilton advocated the creation of a commission to promote business development, encourage new inventions and "afford such other aids to those objectives as may be generally designated by law." Hamilton concluded with these words:

> In countries where there is great private wealth much may be effected by the voluntary contributions of patriotic individuals, but in a community situated like that of the United States, the public purse must supply the deficiency of private resource. In what can it be so useful, as in promoting and improving the efforts of industry?[1]

The federal commission envisioned by Hamilton was never established. But state-level government was already seeking to protect and support industrial growth; Hamilton's model had been the Pennsylvania Society for the Promotion of Manufacturers and Useful Arts.

Supporting business was soon to become an important activity of the government in Washington.

The close relationship between business and government is in some ways a logical outgrowth of U.S. political and economic systems. Louis W. Koenig, a noted authority on U.S. presidents, said, "Presidents as a lot assume that harmony and confidence between government and business are profitable to both." Maintaining that even Franklin Roosevelt, always so quick to attack "economic royalists," was in fact a true friend of business, Koenig pronounces: "No president can be said to be antibusiness."[2]

The Constitution deliberately left some important public functions in the hands of the private sector. Political economist Charles E. Lindblom has noted that job creation, price levels, production, and responsibility for growth and economic security are considered functions primarily of the private sector and only secondarily, if at all, of the public sector. He notes that "Government officials cannot be indifferent to how well business performs its functions. . . . Economic distress can bring down a government. A major function of government, therefore, is to see to it that businessmen perform their tasks."[3]

Politicians must be elected and, they hope, later reelected. Their interest in a strong economy is central to their personal success, since full employment and a healthy economy are among the first concerns of all political constituencies.

Consequently, it is not surprising that over the years those in government have undertaken a variety of programs to support and encourage business and industrial growth. Many of these programs have been government's responsibilities for so long that we take them for granted, for example, road building, weather forecasting, and mail delivery. Yet these responsibilities are crucial to enterprise. Though others are more directly supportive—as in federal financial aid to small business—they are often thought of as only temporary measures.

Government support of business does not square well with the traditional political ideology of the United States, one tenet of which is that business should operate without such assistance. Consequently, the public can be quick to deny that government support programs exist for the private sector.

## GOVERNMENT ACTIVITY ON BEHALF OF BUSINESS

Government activities in support of business and industry come under five headings:

1. Infrastructure creation and maintenance
2. Support of research and development
3. Assistance to new and developing industries
4. Purchases
5. Sales promotion and data bank maintenance

### Infrastructure Responsibilities

Although primary responsibility for production and job creation has been vested in the private sector from the earliest days of this republic, government has always been responsible for some maintenance functions that are crucial to the operations of the economy. One of government's first public works projects was building roads and canals to stimulate commerce or, in some places, simply to make it possible. The capital construction functions of government have been expanding ever since. Building and maintaining roads, interstate highways, waterways, airports, and air navigational systems are examples of the continuing infrastructure responsibilities of government. The Congressional Budget Office estimates that the federal government share of capital infrastructure costs, both construction and maintenance, is close to $25 billion a year.[4] Given the pressing need for maintenance and repair, that figure is likely to grow substantially in coming years.

But these are only the most visible functions of government. The Constitution protects private property rights, a concept that goes to the heart of our free enterprise ideology. Patent, trademark, and copyright protection by government are critical components of our economic system.

Another infrastructure responsibility is reflected in the role the federal government takes in monetary and financial markets: maintaining the safe money and equity markets that are necessary to a viable economy. Much of this infrastructure work of government is economic regulation, as discussed in the previous chapter.

## Research and Development

For several years the federal government has funded from 45 to 50 percent of the research and development carried out in the United States, spending more than $50 billion a year.[5] The FY 1987 budget proposed by President Reagan included R&D expenditures of $63 billion, a 16 percent increase over the previous year. Government bears this large share of total R&D costs for a variety of reasons, one being government's ability to raise substantial amounts of investment capital and commit it for a long time. Most corporations are not able to put off return on investment long enough to make large R&D expenditures feasible. Government also supports R&D because of the results are often beneficial to many companies; single firms cannot be expected to be so magnanimous.

About half of the federal R&D expenditure is in aerospace and more than one-quarter is in electrical equipment. The remainder is allocated in a variety of areas, such as health, energy, education, and the natural sciences. In recent years about 80 percent of federal R&D expenditures have been made by the Department of Defense, the second largest share by NASA, and the remainder by other agencies.

President Reagan's former science advisor, George A. Keyworth II, points to a National Science Foundation program begun in 1984 as an encouraging example of the way business and government can work together to develop new technologies and encourage U.S. competitiveness. The program facilitates collaborative research between corporations and universities. Keyworth sees joint ventures as a challenge to the view that profit-driven corporations "contaminate" universities and rob them of their independence. He writes: "The attitude that 'working together' is a synonym for 'conspiracy against the public interest' must change."[6]

## Financial Assistance

The federal government has saved some companies in financial straits through loans or other devices. The loan programs that rescued the Chrysler and Lockheed corporations and the First Continental Bank of Chicago are dramatic examples. These government intrusions in the market were extremely controversial and probably very costly.

But the magnitude of a Chrysler failure, the loss to defense production caused by a bankrupt Lockheed Corporation, or the impact on financial markets if First Continental had folded made the three interventions seem necessary, if not essential, to government analysts.

Government more commonly assists new or expanding industries. In the early part of the century, the old Post Office Department supported and sustained the burgeoning aircraft and airline industries. By placing the first large order for airplanes, the department provided the initial capital necessary for the industry to begin production. The department assisted in the construction of the first airports, trained the first pilots, and began systematic air transport service. After about ten years the department sold its planes and contracted with the airline industry to carry mail. In the early years airlines were heavily subsidized; today the subsidy continues in modified forms, primarily benefiting some of the small feeder airlines.[7]

A similar pattern of government encouragement occurred in the aerospace industry. Government took the lead in organizing the space program by funding and coordinating a major government-industry collaboration. In recent years the Reagan administration has encouraged private-sector launches and other space activities. A new group of industries has emerged as a result of this collaboration. From mundane devices like fishing nets and special paints to sophisticated high-tech equipment, the commercialization program administered by NASA has become a source of product ideas for both new and developed industries.

A congressional study divided financial aid to industry into three categories: (1) direct spending, such as funding for the development of new technologies, (2) credit programs, including the programs of the Export-Import Bank and the Small Business Administration, and (3) government tax expenditures.[8]

In this revealing study the Congressional Budget Office claimed that the greatest amount of aid to business was through tax expenditures: revenue losses that result from government giving special tax breaks to particular categories of taxpayers. An investment tax credit for industry is one example. Such tax credits to business in 1984 alone amounted to $60 billion of the government's tax expenditures. Most of these tax advantages for business disappeared in the 1986 tax reform legislation. In 1985 and early 1986 their importance to some companies was evident in the aggressive lobbying on Capitol Hill against tax reform.

The Congressional Budget Office found that the second largest category of federal support to business was $13.7 billion in 1984 in direct spending on research grants and other types of grants. Areas as diverse as mining, transportation, agriculture, and aeronautics received such funding. The third channel of support to industry—costing about $8.8 billion in 1984—was through credit programs covering defaults and the costs of loans and loan guarantees. Several items were not included in the tally. For example, the figures do not include housing subsidies, certain R&D programs that were not industry-specific, Department of Defense purchases of goods and services, and some tax credits that benefit individuals but immediately benefit certain industries as well. By allowing the tax deductibility of interest on home mortgages, for example, the federal government did not collect in 1984 nearly $28 billion that it might otherwise have collected—a major boost to the home-building industries.

### Government Purchases

Since the mid–1960s the federal government has been spending between 19 and 25 percent of the gross national product. A large portion of that amount goes to the private sector through direct purchasing. In 1983 U.S. industries shipped over $114 billion in goods and services, under contract or subcontract, to the federal government. That figure represents over 17 percent of all shipments made by U.S. companies. Some industries shipped more than others to the government. The electrical and electronic equipment manufacturers sold over 21 percent of their output to government, and the transportation equipment industry over 58 percent.[9]

For some industries, particularly in their formative years, government contracts were essential to survival. This was especially true in high-tech fields. As recently as 1962 the government's share of shipments from the U.S. semiconductor industry was 100 percent. That share dropped to 94 percent in 1963 and has continued to drop. Today it is in the range of 10 to 20 percent.[10]

### Sales Promotion and Data Collection

Several federal departments take major responsibility for export trade promotion of both agricultural and manufactured products.

The Departments of State and Commerce and Agriculture as well as the Export-Import Bank are primarily responsible for these promotional activities. State and Commerce devote large shares of their resources to the promotion of international trade. Both departments maintain staffs in foreign capitals to produce market feasibility surveys and financial or political analyses as well as to provide assistance to businesses on specific trade problems. The federal government, mainly through the White House Office of the Special Trade Representative, represents U.S. companies abroad on trade and related matters. Its purpose is to facilitate the export of U.S. products and to create a fair, competitive environment for goods imported into this country.

In addition to these visible and quantifiable efforts, a myriad of less obvious, sometimes informal government activities are of great value to business and industry The Department of Commerce and other agencies collect demographic and income data used frequently by business in market analysis. Other government data, such as the leading economic indicators and some specialized consumer data, are used for planning and investment purposes. In 1985 the federal outlay for statistical services was nearly $1.5 billion.

## INDUSTRIAL POLICY: PROS AND CONS

With such a broad array of government programs, from restrictive regulation to encouraging assistance, it is little wonder that such diverse groups as labor, agriculture, and the auto industry are suggesting ways to order and plan these government interventions. Support for discussions of industrial policy issues has been voiced by various political activists and corporate executives. There is, however, little or no agreement among them on what those policies should be or how they should be carried out.

All agree that we need an industrial policy, and agree that there are two reasons why. First, government has been active historically in shaping the industrial sector. Today some say that those activities are intrusive and badly coordinated. Government's role could at least be made more effective. Second, increased competition from abroad is more intense and sophisticated than ever; some believe that we must organize ourselves better to compete more forcefully with countries that have different political and economic systems.

Although several proposals have been presented in Congress for one type of industrial policy or another, the congressional response to the more extreme suggestions is at best skeptical and more often negative. The prevailing view is that little is wrong with the structure of the U.S. economy, and that it can still compete effectively if left alone by government. Limiting government to making macroeconomic policy is about all the industrial policy many people think we need.

This argument contends that if federal deficits could be brought under control, interest rates would fall and so would the value of the dollar. Our exports would then increase, the economy would enjoy a recovery, and there would be no need for government to intervene any further. Indeed, further government intervention might be costly and troublesome and would create more problems than it could resolve. Government intervention has already introduced unwanted distortions in domestic markets. Politicians have a tendency to try shoring up older, noncompetitive industries through tariff protection, loans, or other devices. In the long run these hurt the economy, U.S. industry, and eventually the consumer.[11]

One student of U.S. business-government relations, Graham K. Wilson, has noted several instances when government and business became too intertwined and the public suffered. Government often caves in to the demands of industry. As examples he cites tax write-offs like the oil depletion allowance, and the trade barriers erected to assist the domestic textile industry.[12]

Whether or not Wilson is correct about the effect of tax write-offs, many believe that the worst case of government intervention is protectionism. Elected officials are under heavy pressure, especially when the economy is weak, to protect domestic industries that are having trouble with foreign competitors. The political attraction of tariff barriers is strong; but the economic effects can be disastrous, especially on consumers in the short run and on the health of the international economic system in the long run. One scholar in international economics has estimated that the quota system limiting Japanese auto imports added about $2,500 to the cost of each Japanese auto purchased in this country in 1984. Domestic auto prices have risen about $1,000 per auto because of the protection extended by the quotas. The cost to U.S. consumers has been nearly $5 billion each year the quotas have been in place.[13]

If industrial policy were to mean simply manipulation of domestic markets and erection of tariff barriers to protect domestic industries, few people would even want to discuss it seriously. An industrial policy used this way would weaken, not strengthen, the competitive position of the U.S. economy. An industrial policy that encouraged only certain special interests to implement their own programs would be a great mistake.

Unfortunately, the dispersed and pluralistic organization of federal decisionmaking processes (described later in this book) and the strength of special interest organizations make such an undesirable outcome a distinct possibility.[14] The U.S. political system tends to reward and protect older, troubled industries that are no longer as efficient as they should be. Politics favors the established, not the risk takers and innovators. Some politicians and entrenched managers argue that the United States should take a strong, centralized approach to industrial planning. Such a policy would be likely to stifle innovation and competitiveness, making growth more difficult.

Edward F. Denison puts the case against a centralized industrial policy succinctly:

> It is fortunate that recent administrations in Washington have had little enthusiasm for another possible area of government action: attempts to identify future "winners" and "losers" among industries. . . . Skepticism about the superiority of government foresight, and recognition that it is troubled industries that exert the strongest political pressures, backstop this attitude.[15]

## EXISTING AND PROPOSED INDUSTRIAL POLICIES

The United States does not have one industrial policy, with a centralized agency of government directing the economy, but it does have industrial *policies* that are important to continued industrial growth. Removing government from its traditional role as a contributor to industrialization is probably not possible and would be a costly mistake even if it were. Robert B. Reich views the split between business and government as an anachronism. "In advanced industrial nations like the United States, drawing . . . sharp distinctions between government and market [business] has long ceased to be useful."[16] The challenge for the United States is to establish government and business policies that will better prepare us for a complex and more competitive future.

Reich and others believe that the United States does have some industrial policies that have been useful over the years. Our tax and export programs have certainly encouraged some industries and discouraged others. They are both difficult to analyze as policies and often subvert each other. Some people deny that these programs reflect policy, but they should and could be so formulated and then used to our competitive advantage.

George C. Lodge and William C. Crum of the Harvard Business School look at U.S. industrial policy this way:

> Our tradition ... has, ironically, created a very large interventionary and expensive government. It has also spawned a vast array of transfer payments, subsidies and credit programs, as well as environmental, tax, and monetary policies that restrain savings, investment, and industrial growth, but whose impact on U.S. competitiveness is seldom fully assessed. As federal policies increasingly affect America's trade prospects, the government now must recognize all the consequences of its actions, choose priorities among many desirable goals and create a consensus to implement its choices.[17]

Lodge and Crum ask, "To ensure America's future competitiveness, should not we distinguish ... between tobacco growing, semi-conductor manufacturing and shoemaking?"[18]

In recent years state governments have been more active than the federal government in pursuing a type of industrial policy. They have encouraged certain industries to locate within their states and have made greater contributions to research and training in high technology for the benefit of industries in that field. Some states have set aside land for research parks and have made venture capital available by tapping resources accumulating in state pension funds. It is politically easier for the states than for the federal government to make choices among companies. And the cumulative effect of fifty states competing for business is likely to be less harmful than what would happen if the federal government picked winners and losers for the nation as a whole.[19]

More and more people agree that the United States should not and could not run an industrial policy planning system through a central government bureaucracy. The federal government structure does not lend itself to the sort of decisionmaking required by such a planning system. Indeed, it is doubtful that a centralized industrial policy works well in any country. The emerging consensus is toward developing a dispersion of industrial policies in the United States, with these characteristics:

1. Further education for those in business, labor, and government on how our industrial policy systems operate today, including an exchange of information from the experiences of each sector

2. Strategic planning and issues management through cooperative forums involving business, labor, and government

3. Identification of current industrial policies and their impact on industry through asking such questions as, Do our tax codes favor consumption or investment? Do our policies handicap certain industries with greater potential in international marketplaces?

4. Industrial policy decisions made on the reoriented basis of how they might influence our world competitive position

5. A mechanism to coordinate and rationalize all government policies that affect industry, either positively or negatively

This kind of sorting-out process has support across the political spectrum. Some continue to argue that such an approach is too modest and that the country needs a government-led shot in the arm to stimulate competitiveness, similar to what the Apollo project did for space research and exploration. There are proposals in Congress, for example, to create an industrial development bank run by the government. It would grant loans to businesses at artificially low rates. Loan decisions would be made by a board representing business, labor, academia, and government. Presently, there seems little chance of passage for this or other legislation that would give government a centralized and more direct role in the economy.

Proposals to create an industrial policy forum, or to restructure the Department of Commerce into a Department of Trade, seem more likely to pass. These are low-key and facilitative approaches to industrial policy. In the long run an advisory role for government is more likely to find favor in the United States.

A conservative political analyst, Kevin Phillips, has outlined an agenda for an industrial policy. It includes changes in federal trade organization, policy, and law; reform of lobbying, tax law, and labor management relations; and new federal programs to support education, research, and technology.[20]

It might surprise some that conservatives would also advocate a more active role for government in its relations with business and industry. As Phillips points out, however, his proposals are in line with the oldest of American traditions in business and government relations. As support grows across the political spectrum for a more systematic approach to government-industry relations, so might discussion and action increase over the next few years. The adversarial relationship between government and business—which the public sees most often—will probably subside somewhat as both parties realize the opportunities for cooperative action. Business executives will continue to find government an indispensable partner: on everything from sales and tax treatment to the no less important areas of R&D, loans, and data collection.

## NOTES

1. Alexander Hamilton, *A Report on Manufactures*, presented to Congress on December 5, 1791.
2. Louis W. Koenig, *The Chief Executive*, 4th ed. (New York: Harcourt Brace Jovanovich, 1981), p. 266.
3. Charles E. Lindblom, *Politics and Markets* (New York: Basic Books, 1977), pp. 172–73.
4. This figure includes federal contributions to highways, public transit, wastewater treatment, water resources, air traffic control, airports, and municipal water supply. Congressional Budget Office, from data supplied by several federal agencies.
5. Congressional Budget Office, *Federal Support for R&D and Innovation* (Washington, D.C.: U.S. Government Printing Office, 1984).
6. G.A. Keyworth II, "Cooperation Aids Competitiveness," *Wall Street Journal*, 9 December 1985.
7. For an interesting history of the Postal Service and aviation, see Page Shamburger, *Tracks Across the Sky: The Story of the Pioneers of the U.S. Airmail* (Philadelphia: J. B. Lippincott, 1964).
8. Congressional Budget Office, *Federal Support of U.S. Business* (Washington, D.C.: U.S. Government Printing Office, 1984), ch. 2.
9. Department of Commerce, Bureau of the Census, *Current Industrial Reports—Shipments to Federal Government Agencies, 1983*, MA 175 (Washington, D.C.: U.S. Government Printing Office, 1984).
10. See Richard R. Nelson, ed., *Government and Technical Progress: A Cross-Industry Analysis* (New York: Pergamon Press, 1982), p. 63.

11.  See Robert Z. Lawrence, *Can America Compete?* (Washington, D.C.: The Brookings Institution, 1984) for an extended discussion of this point of view.

12.  Graham K. Wilson, *Business and Politics: A Comparative Introduction* (Chatham, N.J.: Chatham House, 1985). ch. 1.

13.  Robert W. Crandall, "Detroit Rode Quotas to Prosperity," *Wall Street Journal*, 29 January 1986.

14.  Charles L. Schultze, who has much experience in high-level government positions, makes this argument in his article, "Industrial Policy: A Dissent," *Brookings Review* 2, no. 1 (1983): 3.

15.  Edward F. Denison, *Trends in American Economic Growth, 1929–1982* (Washington, D.C.: The Brookings Institution, 1985), p. 61.

16.  Robert B. Reich, *The Next American Frontier* (New York: Quadrangle/ New York Times Books, 1983), p. 5.

17.  George C. Lodge and William C. Crum, "The Pursuit of Remedies," in Bruce R. Scott and George C. Lodge, eds., *U.S. Competitiveness in the World Economy* (Boston: Harvard Business School Press, 1985), p. 496.

18.  Ibid., p. 497.

19.  See Edward V. Regan and Bruno J. Mauer, *Innovations in Industrial Competitiveness at the State Level*, Report to the President's Commission on Industrial Competitiveness (New York: Chemical Bank, December 1984).

20.  Kevin T. Phillips, *Staying on Top: The Business Case for a National Industrial Strategy* (New York: Random House, 1984), p. 81.

# 5 THE MANAGEMENT AND MANAGERS OF GOVERNMENT

Changes in current industrial policies and the creation of new ones will directly involve the government's core of managers, the civil service. Our success in implementing any type of industrial policy largely depends on the quality and skill of these people.

Managing government programs is primarily the responsibility of the bureaucracy: the nonpolitical career public service. For business executives and others who deal with government, these are the key people. Often criticized—sometimes with justification—civil servants are not well known to the public. They are a large and diverse group. Who they are, where they work, how they operate, what their pay and incentive systems are, and what type of training they receive are important questions to answer for those who seek to influence government policymaking.

## HOW MANY AND WHERE?

The number of civilians employed by the federal government—about 2.9 million—has not changed significantly since 1967. Data on the mix of agencies they work for and the numbers employed by each agency can be surprising. The agencies with the most civilian workers—the Department of Defense, the Postal Service, and the Veterans

Administration—employ about 2 million of the 2.9 million total, or about 70 percent of the government's civilian work force.

Only about 355,000, under 12 percent of the total civilian work force, are employed in the Washington metropolitan area. The federal government is a broadly decentralized bureaucracy. Most of its employees work in the ten regional centers, in other U.S. cities, and around the world. The Washington metropolitan area is only the tip of the employment iceberg.

The concern that business executives often voice about a huge, centralized, and growing federal bureaucracy is largely unwarranted. Measured against GNP or population growth, bureaucracy has been declining in size over the past several years. In 1955 there were 14.3 federal employees for every 1,000 people in the United States, and today that figure is down to about 12 (see Table 5-1). Even the real figures show no significant change in well over a decade. (During the Reagan administration the mix has changed, however, with an increase of over 100,000 in the Defense Department and a decrease of slightly less than 100,000 in the domestic agencies.[1]) With almost 70 percent of the federal work force employed by three departments and almost 90 percent working outside the Washington area, it is difficult to substantiate claims that the federal government is overcentralized.

Figures on only federal employment do not accurately reflect the size of the federal government, for these numbers do not include the multitude of people dependent upon the federal government for a job. Several million people are not on the federal payroll but derive their salaries from government grants and contracts. These workers include those employed by state and local governments as a result of federal programs, university faculty on government research projects, and employees of private businesses with government contracts. The Department of Defense estimated in FY 1985 that 2.7 million people "receive salaries funded by DOD through research and service contracts and DOD procurement and construction activities."[2]

The big growth area in public employment is in state and local governments. In 1984 the total number employed was about 13.5 million (see Table 5-2). Nearly 4 million people work for the fifty state governments; that is 1 million more than the number of civilians in federal employment. And 9.4 million people work for cities, counties, towns, and villages across the country. The number of state and local employees has been growing rapidly. Whereas the number

Table 5-1.  Government Employment and Population, 1955–85.

| Fiscal Year | Government Employment | | | Population | |
|---|---|---|---|---|---|
| | Federal Executive Branch[a] (thousands) | State and Local Governments (thousands) | All Governmental Units (thousands) | Federal as Percent of All Governmental Units | Total U.S. (thousands) | Federal Employment per 1,000 Population |
| 1955 | 2,371 | 4,728 | 7,099 | 33.4 | 165,931 | 14.3 |
| 1960[b] | 2,371 | 6,073 | 8,444 | 28.1 | 180,671 | 13.1 |
| 1965 | 2,496 | 7,683 | 10,179 | 24.5 | 194,303 | 12.8 |
| 1970[b] | 2,944 | 9,869 | 12,813 | 23.0 | 205,052 | 14.4 |
| 1975 | 2,848 | 12,114 | 14,962 | 19.0 | 215,973 | 13.2 |
| 1980[b] | 2,821 | 13,542 | 16,363 | 17.2 | 228,279[c] | 12.4 |
| 1985 | 2,964 | 13,743 | 16,707 | 17.7 | 239,440[c] | 12.4 |

a. Covers total end-of-year employment of full-time permanent, temporary, part-time, and intermittent employees in the executive branch, including the Postal Service, and, beginning in 1970, including various disadvantaged youth and worker-trainee programs.

b. Includes temporary employees for the decennial census.

c. On January 1, 1969, 42,000 civilian technicians of the Army and Air Force National Guard were converted by law from state to federal employment status. They are included in the federal employment figures in this table starting with 1970.

Source:  Office of Management and Budget, *Budget for Fiscal Year 1987*, p. I-10.

Table 5-2.  Public Sector Employment as of October 1984.

| | |
|---|---:|
| All governments | 16,435,000 |
| Federal (civilian) | 2,942,000 |
| States | 3,898,000 |
| Countries | 1,872,000 |
| Municipalities | 2,434,000 |
| Townships | 386,000 |
| School districts | 4,387,000 |
| Special districts | 516,000 |

Source: U.S. Bureau of the Census.

of federal employees per 1,000 population has decreased since the early 1950s, the number of state and local employees per 1,000 population has increased in that period by over 120 percent.[3]

Government personnel perform a wide variety of jobs. Employed on the federal level alone is almost every type of skilled or unskilled worker. Over 40 percent of the 16.4 million public employees in this country, however, are working in public school systems, making public education the largest function of the U.S. government in terms of the number of personnel employed.

The regulatory bodies that oversee business practices have far fewer employees than is generally believed. The Security and Exchange Commission, for example, employs 1,900 people. The Federal Trade Commission employs 1,280. Two other agencies important to the business community are the Environmental Protection Agency and the Occupational Safety and Health Administration, which employ 13,940 and 2,318 people, respectively.

At the executive level in the civil service there are around 650 cabinet secretaries, assistant secretaries, and other high-level appointees who require confirmation by the Senate. Below them are approximately 700 lower-level political appointees who do not require Senate confirmation and some 6,200 senior career civil servants. These 7,550 government executives are responsible for managing over 2.2 million civilian personnel. (The Postal Service is not included in these figures.) Guided by the policies of presidential appointees, they administer a budget of more than $990 billion per year.

The 6,200 career civil servants are hired not by the president but by open competition. This corps of experienced career managers and senior professionals (such as scientists and engineers) is the principal support system for federal management. The 700 managers in this group are appointed by cabinet officials and other presidential appointees. They serve at the pleasure of their agency head and are usually replaced after a change in administration.

A study based on interviews with 536 recent presidential appointees showed that they were unhappy with the long delay between the time they agreed to serve and the time of their Senate confirmation. The gap was 6.8 weeks in the Johnson administration; it has risen to 14.6 weeks during the Reagan years. The appointees also criticized the lack of White House assistance. Many claimed they had not received adequate briefings on the president's policy or objectives for the programs they were appointed to supervise. Little wonder that political appointees spend an average of less than two years on the job.[4]

The turnover rate of political appointees is troublesome, but equally difficult is their interest in making a mark on public policy in the short time they serve. The result is that few devote much attention to management, where the rewards of solving problems are meager and usually unnoticed by the public. They concentrate instead on the more grandiose and attractive problems of policy design, which attract public attention. This attitude toward management is frequently frustrating to career civil servants.

One often hears complaints about the relationships between political appointees and civil service managers. But the problems might be more apparent than real. The interviews with appointees revealed relationships between career and political executives are very different from those we generally perceive. Eighty-three percent of the appointees said civil servants were very responsive to their requests and opinions, and an equally high percentage rated career executives as highly competent. Only 6 percent of those interviewed gave negative responses.[5]

## CIVIL SERVICE REFORMS

Problems, some real and others imagined, arising mainly from the uneasy relationship between career and political executives, led to an important 1978 reform in the civil service system. The new civil service plan had two major goals. One was to make the federal bureaucracy more responsive to the goals and policy initiatives of the president and his appointees, while stepping up efforts to protect the civil service from the effects of partisan political activity. This apparent conflict in goals represents a fundamental dilemma in public management: efficiency and expertise versus responsiveness to the legitimate initiatives of our democratically elected leaders. The second goal of civil service reform, related to the first, was to make it easier to reward civil servants who perform well and to penalize or remove those who do not.

The changes mandated by the Civil Service Reform Act included the elimination of the Civil Service Commission, a semi-independent body that for nearly a century had been responsible for most of the personnel functions of the federal government. The commission was replaced by the Office of Personnel Management, an executive agency reporting to the president and responsible now for most personnel matters. The Merit Systems Protection Board is a new semi-independent commission responsible for reviewing employee grievances, including dismissals. The Federal Labor Relations Authority, comparable to the National Labor Relations Board for private-sector employees, was also created.[6]

The most important provision of the new law from a management perspective was the creation of the Senior Executive Service (SES). This is the corps of 6,200 civil service managers discussed earlier. Their salaries range from $60,000 to $72,000 (as of 1986). Managers just below this level are paid between $44,000 and $68,000. Members of the SES may not last as long in their jobs as they did under the old scheme; they can be more easily demoted or removed. But the reform has improved the reward structure by introducing a year-end cash bonus system. As many as 35 percent of all career executives are eligible for a bonus of up to 20 percent of their salaries. Five percent of these top-level managers can receive a "meritorious" rank, carrying a bonus of $10,000; and 1 percent can be designated "distinguished," with an award of $20,000. No person can receive more than one award in a five-year period. Merit pay systems were also adopted for middle-level managers.

These changes, based on private-sector models, are an important restructuring of the rewards, incentives, and penalties for government managers. There have been numerous difficulties in implementing the new law, including the hard task of developing performance standards when profit or loss and similar criteria do not apply. Yet this reformed system could create a new environment that would profoundly alter the way government is managed.

The average length of service for senior government managers is 22.4 years—a substantial tenure in the public service. Political executives, on the other hand, remain public employees for less than three years. A recent survey of 1,200 career executives asked why they remained in public service. Over three-fourths answered that it was "the work itself; the opportunity to have an impact on public affairs."[7]

Since World War II the federal government has shifted away from direct delivery of services to third party contracts: with consulting firms, universities, other not-for-profit organizations, and state and local governments. Charles Levine of the Congressional Research Service asserts that "while the popular image of the federal government is one of acres of clerks processing piles of forms, in reality the federal workforce is approaching the structure of a research and development firm."[8] Levine cites statistics from 1983: 55 percent of federal civilian employees had some college training and 16 percent had done postgraduate work. Almost 22,000 had Ph.D's, over 150,000 had master's degrees, and 15,532 were attorneys.

The shift away from service delivery is one of the important reasons for the slow growth in the size of the federal bureaucracy. Today federal employees plan, develop, and oversee policy while others, under contract or similar arrangement, carry it out.

## COMPARING BENEFITS

One question that comes up frequently in business circles is about the federal retirement system. There are several different retirement systems in the civil service. Law enforcement officials, members of Congress, congressional employees, air traffic controllers, and others receive slightly more liberal benefits than those on the standard government retirement system. The military retirement system is, of course, quite different from all others.

Several study groups have compared the federal retirement system with those in the private sector. The conclusion drawn is that civil service retirement annuities are not seriously out of line with pension plans of large corporations. Federal employees and the agencies they work for each pay 7 percent of salaries into the retirement system.

Benefits and retirement eligibility are calculated on the basis of a formula: for example, employees with thirty years of service are eligible to retire at age fifty-five at about 56 percent of their final salary. Most civil servants, however, are over sixty-one when they retire. Those who entered federal service before 1984 did not participate in the social security system. Private-sector employees covered by the average private pension plan and social security after thirty years of employment receive pensions equaling about 57 percent of their final salary; the social security portion, about 15 percent, is not taxable.

Comparing private- and public-sector compensation packages is difficult. Most studies conclude that white-collar govemment workers have earned less than their private-sector counterparts since 1977. Most private employees pay a larger share of health insurance premiums, and the private plans offer more extensive coverage. The same is generally true for life insurance benefits and payments. Federal employees receive one less holiday per year than those in the private sector but have more generous annual leave provisions.[9]

The major attraction of the federal scheme is that for two decades federal retirement benefits have been indexed to inflation. Adjustments were made every six months during the first decade; since 1981 they have been made annually. Given the substantial rise in the inflation index in the late 1970s and early 1980s, indexing has become a desirable feature of the federal retirement system for those participating in it. For the last few years many private employers have made cost-of-living adjustments in the pensions of their retired employees. But most companies base future annuities of current employees on a combination of social security (which is indexed to inflation), the return on investment from employer contributions, and tax-deferred employee contributions. A 1984 survey by Hay Associates showed that when pay *and* benefits of federal employees are compared with those in the private sector, the total compensation of federal employees is 7.2 percent *lower*.[10]

The number of federal civil servants terminated or fired is a controversial topic that the public seems to be unusually interested in. Although published statistics suggest that very few federal employees are actually fired, this conclusion is not accurate. The misconception is caused by flaws in the statistical and reporting processes.

It certainly is possible to fire federal workers, although the process for doing so is more cumbersome than the process in the private sector. Somewhere between 10,000 and 12,000 employees (not including U.S. Postal Service employees) are fired for cause or involuntarily separated from federal employment each year. This figure has been remarkably consistent over the past decade.[11] It does not include those who are encouraged to leave or retire early. For a bureaucracy of over 2 million people, this is a low but not insignificant number of forced terminations. The total number of separations is much higher; in 1985 it was 545,000 people, or over 18 percent of all federal civilian employees.[12]

## BUREAUCRACY UNDER ATTACK

The federal bureaucracy today is a large, complex institution subject to constant criticism. Even presidents seeking reelection will exhort the public with examples of wild bureaucratic excess committed, ironically enough, by the agencies for which they are ultimately responsible. They speak of ending waste and inefficiency in government bureaucracy by reducing the number of employees and increasing efficiency in operations. Unfortunately, such goals are rarely achieved, often because the reform plans are based on erroneous assumptions.

Candidate Jimmy Carter played the bureaucracy numbers game when he ran for president. One of his campaign brochures claimed that as governor of Georgia he had eliminated 278 of the 300 agencies in Georgia's bureaucracy. As president, he promised to reduce what he said were 1,900 federal agencies to 200. After the election, reorganization planning was a major activity of the Carter administration. In preparing for the reorganization, Carter counted 2,103 government agencies in operation. This grossly exaggerated figure included 1,185 advisory committees and 129 interagency and interdepartmental committees. Reducing the number of federal agencies can be just a political maneuver. One simply counts every little commission or committee (generally these are not staffed and have little or no budget), then abolishes or consolidates some of them. Then one can claim a reduction in the number of government agencies.

In the 1980 campaign, candidates Carter and Reagan differed in most respects, but they shared a distaste for the bureaucracy and both spoke against it. President Reagan continues to denounce the federal bureaucracy, referring to it as "puzzle palaces on the Potomac."

Such repeated attacks have made the average citizen quite skeptical about the role of government in society. Public criticism of government is healthy for a democracy, but too much skepticism can quickly induce a dangerous condition of self-fulfilling prophecy. With the public constantly exposed to criticism of the government bureaucracy, it is not surprising when national polls reflect a low regard for it. A Harris poll indicated in 1966 that 41 percent of those polled had a great deal of confidence in the people running the federal government. In 1976 this figure had fallen to 11 percent. By the end of 1985 the confidence level had increased to 19 percent, but this was far short of the 1966 figure. Antibusiness sentiment has also been rising. Since the late 1960s it has been more prevalent than antigovernment views. In a 1966 poll, 55 percent expressed a great deal of confidence in major corporations, but by 1985 this figure had tumbled to 17 percent.[13] The polls reveal a substantial erosion of public confidence in both institutions.

Faulting public bureaucracies seems to have become a feature of modern political life. The American public has responded positively to politicians who excoriate bureaucrats for lack of judgment, foresight, intelligence, and management skills. There certainly have been many instances of bureaucratic ineptitude, some of them extreme, but public bureaucrats are easy targets.

There is often a gap between our attitude toward the larger bureaucracy and our opinion of individual public servants. For example, the public seems to dislike the Postal Service but likes their local postal workers. Polls taken of people visiting government offices show very high levels of satisfaction with the responsiveness of government employees. Yet the public holds with surprising tenacity to the view that public bureaucracies are inefficient, wasteful, and unresponsive.[14] A major study of public opinion polls over several years concludes: "Most people describe government actions to control or regulate private activities as inefficient, often corrupt, and overly costly; yet when 'push comes to shove,' they still want the government to regulate business, labor, and other private organizations."[15]

Bureaucracy certainly needs to be constantly improved and reformed. It is particularly important to keep pressure on bureaucracy because it is not, like business, subject to the competitive influence of the marketplace. On the other hand, using bureaucracy as a scapegoat for complex social problems can lead to demagoguery and simplistic solutions. Bureaucracy-baiting has already contributed to a serious deterioration of public support for government. The public's pessimism provides an opening for quick-fix demagogues arguing that the nation's problems could be solved if only *they* were given the chance.

In the last several years the morale problem in the top levels of the senior service has become intense. It is partly attributable to budget cuts, forced retirements, and administrative difficulties, but another reason is the public's low esteem for the profession. The survey of 1,200 career executives referred to earlier revealed that 70 percent think the "public image of federal workers" is "more reason for leaving than staying" in public service. A separate survey asked 800 career executives to rank the recognition and respect accorded career executives in the last five administrations. On a scale of 1 to 7 with 7 being the highest, the rankings were: Johnson, 5.5; Nixon, 5.3; Ford, 5.3; Carter, 4.5; and Reagan, 4.1[16]

Norman Ornstein, a senior staff member of the American Enterprise Institute and an observer of Congress, recently wrote that we are in danger of losing competent bureaucrats because of the popular political sport of thoughtless criticism. He suggests that we establish a system of Nobel-type prizes to encourage the best and draw public attention to valuable accomplishments.[17]

Those in business should take the time to look behind criticisms of bureaucratic performance and determine whether there are good reasons for the government procedures and responses that the business community finds so repugnant. Red tape, for example, is sometimes the result of procedural requirements forced on public bureaucracies by interest groups, some of which represent business itself. The pursuit of fairness often demands that certain open, cumbersome, time-consuming procedures be followed. Public bureaucrats are usually more opposed to these requirements than anyone else—they have to live with them every day. One person's red tape is another person's idea of fairness, equity, and good government. Nevertheless, cumbersome and costly bureaucratic procedures that do not benefit or protect anyone should be fought and changed.

## NOTES

1. U.S. Office of Personnel Management, *Monthly Federal Report of Civilian Employment*, September 1985.

2.  Office of the Secretary of Defense, *Annual Report to Congress*, 1984.
3.  Office of Management and Budget, *U.S. Government, Budget for Fiscal Year 1987, Special Analysis*, p. I–12.
4.  National Academy of Public Administration, *Leadership in Jeopardy: The Fraying of the Presidential Appointments System*, The Final Report of the Presidential Appointee Project, November 1985, pp. 11, 19.
5.  Ibid., p. 29.
6.  Charles H. Levine, ed. *The Unfinished Agenda for Civil Service Reform: Implications of the Grace Commission Report* (Washington, D.C.: The Brookings Institution, 1985), p. 69, and Bernard Rosen, "Effective Continuity of U.S. Government Operations in Jeopardy," *Public Administration Review* 43 (1983): 383–92.
7.  U.S. Merit Systems Protection Board, *1984 Report on the Senior Executive Service* (Washington, D.C.: U.S. Government Printing Office, December 1984).
8.  Levine, "The Federal Government in the Year 2000: Administrative Legacies of the Reagan Years," *Public Administration Review* 46 (1986): 195–206.
9.  General Accounting Office, *Comparison of Federal and Private Sector Pay and Benefits*, 4 September 1985.
10. Cited in news release, Committee on Post Office and Civil Service, U.S. House Representatives, 5 December 1984.
11. U.S. Office of Personnel Management, "Discharge and Related Data, FY 1984."
12. U.S. Office of Personnel Management, Office of Workforce Information, September 1985.
13. The Harris Survey, "Confidence in Major Institutions Down" (New York: Louis Harris and Associates, 16 December 1985).
14. Charles T. Goodsell, *The Case for Bureaucracy*, 2d ed. (Chatham, N.J.: Chatham House, 1986).
15. Seymour Martin Lipset and William Schneider, *The Confidence Gap: Business, Government and Labor in the Public Mind* (New York: The Free Press, 1983), p. 379.
16. Reported in Federal Executive Institute Alumni Association, *FEIAA Newsletter* (January 1985).
17. Norman J. Ornstein, "Stop Bashing Our Bureaucrats," *Newsweek*, 1 July 1985.

# 6 DECISIONMAKING SYSTEMS AND THE CORPORATE LOBBYIST

All levels of government in the United States deal with large and complex problems. The decisionmaking structures that address these problems mirror the complexity, but not always the size, of the issues to be resolved. To prevent governmental power from being concentrated in only a few hands, the Constitution established a decisionmaking structure that deliberately pits institutions, and sometimes individuals, against each other. The Constitution most certainly does not provide a modern management structure for government decisionmaking.

It should not be surprising that the large institutions of government do not always act together or have coordinated functions. Government programs are extremely diverse. Although one hopes, for example, that defense decisions and agricultural decisions do not conflict with each other, at the same time it is reasonable to expect decisionmaking in these areas to be made separately. Similarly, the Veterans Administration, the Public Health Service, and the National Park Service may all provide public services, but cannot be expected to share powers over their separate responsibilities.

This inherent lack of coordination between widely disparate government programs is just one reason that real decisionmaking goes on in the smaller government systems. They are more compact, and much easier to deal with than the large institutions created by the Constitution: Congress, the presidency, and the courts.

69

For individuals who want to participate effectively in government decisionmaking, the first task is to identify these smaller systems where most decisions are made. The nation's political leaders and the media focus attention on the large issues like new arms control proposals, major shifts in expenditures, tax reform proposals, and the size and control of the federal deficit. These issues occupy center stage in American public life. Eighty to 90 percent of operational decisions, however, are made by a few people in relatively low-level positions in the executive and congressional branches. They are identifiable and fairly predictable in their operations.

## DEFINING PROGRAM INTERESTS

Government decisionmaking systems are narrowly focused. There is no single decisionmaking system for something as broad or abstract as "foreign affairs" or "trade policy" or "agriculture policy." These are important but amorphous political ideas with little operational meaning. The trade and agricultural policies of the United States are each the sum of dozens of programs that are enforced by specific statutes and agency regulations. Trade policy, for instance, covers export promotion, import restrictions, loan guarantees, national security programs, and even fiscal and monetary programs that affect the value of the dollar. Health policy covers hospital construction, cancer research, medical school education, drug licensing, communicable disease control, and dozens of other specific programs. Instead of looking for an operational decisionmaking system for "agricultural policy," business executives should find the decision systems for specific agricultural programs, like price supports for various commodities, soil conservation, meat and grain inspection, and food stamps.

These systems wherein the operating decisions of government are actually made are small and predictable. There are nearly as many of them as there are groups of related programs they implement; a reasonable estimate would be 800 to 1,000.[1] The effective corporate representative learns quickly to differentiate between general policy discussions—which are interesting but usually unproductive—and program-focused activities taking place within these decision systems.

## COMPONENTS OF DECISIONMAKING SYSTEMS

Each decisionmaking system has several sets of actors. In Congress at least two subcommittees are responsible for each government program: one in the House and one in the Senate (Figure 6-1). These are the authorization committees. They are responsible for the legislation that creates a program and exercise oversight functions as a program becomes operational. Appropriations subcommittees are also part of the decision system. Before the work of the authorization committee can be implemented, the appropriations committee must recommend funds for each new program.

Every government program must go twice through the entire legislative cycle, including presidential signature. The authorization cycle creates or reauthorizes the program; this must happen once every

**Figure 6-1.** A Government Decisionmaking System.

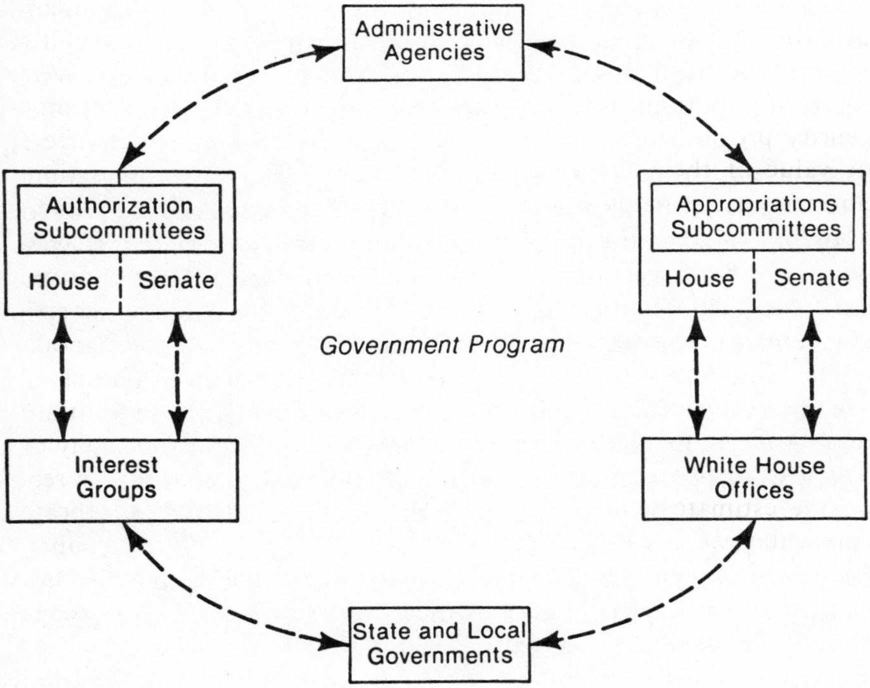

one, two, or three years. An expenditure ceiling is set in the authorizing legislation. The second legislative cycle is the annual appropriations bill for the program. No money can be spent from the U.S.
Treasury until this second bill becomes law. The appropriations bill
may not exceed the ceiling set in the authorization bill.

Very few programs become operational in a hurried or casual
fashion since the legislative wheel must turn twice and each cycle is
marked by numerous checkpoints. Those inside and outside of government must expend considerable resources, pressure, and time to
make a program operational. Government programs can be weak,
ineffective, inappropriate, misguided, and costly, but several major
institutions push them through this lengthy and complicated process
that converts an idea or proposal into law. The assumption is generally wrong that a bad program (that is, one we disagree with) is the
product of a few misguided government officials acting alone.

Both congressional and bureaucratic officials are crucial to the development and operation of programs, but they seldom act without
the guidance and pressure exerted by powerful political groups and
social forces. This is why a program, once started, is so difficult to
stop. Many people support a program initially, and as time passes
they increase and solidify their support. When support is weak in the
beginning and fails to grow, the program usually disappears. The
auto seat belt interlock system regulation, which required that belts
be fastened before auto engines could be started, was proposed and
then withdrawn within one model year. There was little support for
it anywhere after the initial surge of interest. The program to have
banks withhold taxes on interest paid to depositors suffered the same
fate. The lack of public support made it easier for banking interests
to convince Congress to kill this program.

The president is seldom involved in this level of decisionmaking,
but his staff is. The personnel of the Office of Management and Budget (OMB) are involved, as are the people who work for the Domestic
Policy Council. In addition, both OMB and special assistants to the
president monitor and promote the progress of the president's
agenda in program decisions.

Interest groups are active participants in the decisionmaking systems. The number of groups involved varies from one issue to the
next. If the issue is controversial, many groups will be active; if the
issue is not a high priority on the public agenda, less interest group
participation is likely.

The federal agency is very important in decisionmaking systems. Both political and career agency executives exert power more consistently and more skillfully over time than any others in the process. Just as a good quarterback knows the capabilities of all the players and uses them to best advantage, so does a good agency or bureau chief orchestrate the decisionmaking system. It would be an unusual football game with only the quarterback on the field, and a decisionmaking system would be equally bizarre with only the agency heads operating. Any individual or group in the system can change decisions, and they often do. The agency officials are important (some would say "first among equals"), but they may not be able to control the system well or for very long if they disregard the power located elsewhere in the system and forget how that power is exercised.

Since most federal domestic programs are administered by state and local governments, decisionmaking systems for those programs include state and local legislatures and their bureaucracies. Few domestic programs are funded and administered exclusively by the federal government. Housing, welfare, education, highway, mass transit, and airport programs, for example, are funded in part by Washington but run almost wholly by state and local governments. The Postal Service, veterans' programs, and the federal regulatory programs are among the few exceptions. These programs have little state or local government participation in their management.

## IMPORTANT CHARACTERISTIC OF DECISIONMAKING SYSTEMS

The decision systems of government are generally invisible to the public. The mass media almost always covers the federal government by institution, not by program. The television and radio networks, for example, assign correspondents to the White House, Capitol Hill, and the Pentagon. Only a few mass media reporters are assigned to cover specific programs, and they usually do not follow these programs through decisionmaking systems. Although it is easy to find these systems if one knows where to look, one cannot rely on the mass media as a proper guide to government decisionmaking.

The breadth and depth of control by the decisionmaking systems over their programs is surprising. The participants in the systems create the program through the authorizing legislation, fund it through the appropriating legislation, manage it in the federal agencies, and review its progress through congressional oversight hearings. There are, of course, some reviews from outside of the decisionmaking system. The press, the public interest groups, the General Accounting Office (a congressional agency), and others with direct and competing interests in the program can all act as overseers. Sometimes the courts become involved, but generally only after decisions on an existing program have been challenged in a law suit. But to initiate, modify, fine-tune, or eliminate a program, one always has to contend every step of the way with the people in the decision system governing that program.

Another important characteristic of decisionmaking systems is their low level in the organizational hierarchies. Congress is usually not involved in the decisionmaking process on most programs and neither are the full committees. Power on Capitol Hill is organized like a pyramid, with the subcommittees at the base. About 90 percent of subcommittee actions are upheld by full committees. Actions of a full committee are upheld about 70 percent of the time on the floor of the House or Senate. This means one has a very good chance of predicting the outcome of a decision if one knows how a subcommittee is likely to vote.[2]

The bureau or office involved in the decisionmaking system is a small unit within the executive branch hierarchy. For example, there are almost sixty bureaus, agencies, and centers within the Department of Health and Human Services alone. Cabinet secretaries or their immediate deputies would rarely be involved in more than a few of the decisionmaking systems. Their role is overall coordination, development, and innovation, not specific program activity. The participation of interest groups is common and important, but seldom do the presidents or boards of the groups involve themselves directly; their Washington representatives are the regular participants in government's decision systems.

The president is also an outsider—albeit a powerful one—in the program decisionmaking systems. Presidents have little reason to become directly involved; many programs are controversial and fraught with political dangers. Unless a program involves a major issue—energy, for example—most presidents will keep their hands off because the costs of defeat are greater than the rewards of victory. Presidents are often better advised to deal with the more distant matters of foreign policy. After two years in office President Carter looked weak, as evidenced by his plummeting ratings. His lack of success in several domestic areas called his reelectability into queston. The 1978 Middle East summit breakthrough at Camp David changed things; Carter seemed to become an effective statesman and a powerful president overnight. His ratings went up temporarily, but he was unable to keep them that high in the long run. President Reagan received similar accolades for his handling of the *Achille Lauro* hijacking and its aftermath. Most presidents have been reluctant to get involved in the controversial operations of hundreds of government programs when participating in more dramatic events can have greater political significance.

The actual number of participants in the decisionmaking process is small. Participants in Congress are the chairs of the subcommittees, two or three other subcommittee members, and a handful of staffers. Each decisionmaking system includes about half a dozen subcommittee members, along with a staff of twenty or so. In the agencies the numbers are even smaller. With 90 percent of the federal bureaucracy outside of Washington, a relatively small number of bureaucrats staff the offices in Washington. Consequently, six to ten people near the top of a bureau, usually including the chief, are the active participants. The White House staff is also a relatively small organization. Two or three people in the Office of Management and Budget might be assigned to a specific program area, and two or three on the Domestic Policy Council. Thus there are seldom more than six participants from the White House. The number of interest group participants varies according to the issue, sometimes dramatically. Even here, however, the number of participants is normally not very high.

Ongoing responsibility for each federal program rests in the hands of thirty to fifty key people, a surprisingly small number. The members of the federal bureaucracy, the Washington lobbyist corps, and the Capitol Hill staff are spread rather thin over a large number of programs. And, of course, the federal bureaucracy itself is widely dispersed geographically.

The small number of decisionmaking participants leads to several other important characteristics. The decisionmakers know each other well; they interact almost daily; and many of them have been working together for years. In fact, many have worked in more than one of the institutions in the system. If a job opens up in one of the program offices of the Department of Housing and Urban Development and a dozen people apply, the applicant who has worked on the subcommittee dealing with housing and urban legislation on the Hill is at a real advantage. These people not only know each other well, they also know each other's views on policies affecting the program. Since the group is small and well acquainted, the decisions taken on programs are rarely surprising. Change in these decisionmaking systems does occur regularly, but it is usually incremental and seldom dramatic. This gives government programs some stability and predictability in the often volatile political environment.

There is characteristically a high level of expertise in the decisionmaking systems. Not only are participants usually experts in their field or program area, these systems also draw testimony and support from many outside experts. The formal procedures for congressional committee hearings are designed to tap knowledgeable witnesses from across the country. Interest groups, of course, are also expert in their fields. There are close relationships between interest groups and those appointed to the top jobs in the agencies. For example, the person who runs the National Cancer Institute is almost always a research scientist or physician. The people who run the major education programs for the federal government usually have doctorates in education. Those who head the various bureaus in the Department of Agriculture come from the agricultural community.

Expertise does not guarantee wise decisions. Experts are often true believers; they might exercise sound judgment in their specialities, but cannot see the bigger picture. Developing priorities among conflicting programs is difficult enough for policy experts. Furthermore, a high level of expertise does not ensure that a decisionmaking system uses its information well. Poor use of information is at times more of a problem than not having adequate information in the first place.

## THE ROLE OF CONGRESS IN DECISIONMAKING

Observers have noted that "Congress at work" is congressional committees and subcommittees in action. There are sixteen full, or standing committees in the Senate and twenty-two in the House. These legislative committees do the bulk of congressional business. Membership on these committees is determined by political party; the party with a majority in each house has the majority of seats on each committee. The Republican and Democratic party caucuses decide committee assignments. Once assigned, members usually stay and work their way up the seniority ladder of their committees. There is very little shifting of assignments for reelected members. Should members take a reassignment, they usually go to the bottom of the committee seniority list. In the House each member is assigned to only one committee, while in the Senate a member can serve on up to three committees. Members of either house may also be assigned to select, special, or joint committees.

Committees are divided into subcommittees so there can be a reasonable distribution of the work load. Subcommittee jurisdictions mirror the organization of the bureaucracy. The subcommittees authorize programs and then oversee the bureaus and agencies that implement them. Over a period of years members develop expertise in their subcommittee's activities. Members of Congress also remain on subcommittees once they are assigned to them because seniority usually determines the power structure of the subcommittee. The longer they remain on the subcommittee, the more likely they are to become chairperson, with power to appoint subcommittee staff, schedule hearings, and wield power in the decisionmaking system. Some chairpersons are more powerful than others: Carl Vinson of Georgia dominated armed services activities and Daniel Flood of Pennsylvania was extremely influential in even the routine management of the Office of Education.

The powerful chair position makes it difficult for leaders in the House and Senate to organize and run committees and subcommittees. The Speaker of the House and the majority leader of the Senate operate through, rather than around, the committee and subcommittee chairs. The principal tasks of the congressional leaders are organizing the party to conduct its legislative business, scheduling legislation for floor debate, collecting and distributing relevant information, ensuring attendance for votes, and serving as a liaison with the White House on some of the key policy issues being considered by the president.[3]

Congress is often thought of as a relatively conservative institution that is slow to change. Over the past fifteen years, however, Congress has adopted numerous reforms, most of them tending to democratize and decentralize the two houses. Some observers believe the reform movement went too far. Power is now so diffuse, they say, that it is extremely difficult for the leadership to exert the influence and impose the sanctions necessary to move issues to the decisionmaking stage.

Many factors contributed to these sweeping reforms, but among the major ones were change in membership, decline of the political parties, and better management of Congress. More than 60 percent of the House and Senate membership has been elected since 1974. These younger members became impatient with the rigid seniority system, which vested enormous power in the committee and sub-committee chairs. As a result they banded together, irrespective of party, and worked to create more flexibility in the system for chosing committee and subcommittee chairs.

With fewer and fewer members voting party lines in Congress, it has become harder for the leadership to exert party discipline as a means of commanding voting allegiance. More and more members are establishing their independence from some fairly strict party positions. This is most obvious among members who elect to vote one way on domestic issues but another way on foreign policy concerns.

There is a movement under way to better organize and manage Congress. Members are being held more accountable. Stringent financial reporting requirements have been imposed, and caps have been placed on the amount of money members can receive in honoraria payments. Their financial and personal lives are being more heavily scrutinized; some members find the increased attention more than they and their families can tolerate for very long. This is contributing to a high turnover rate.

The major changes enacted by the younger members focused on changing perhaps moribund rules and dispersing more of the power. Congress opened to the public more hearings, conference committee meetings, and bill-markup sessions. Most important, however, were the rule changes that gave individual members more power. Congress placed greater limits on the number of committee and subcommittee assignments a member could have. This automatically opened up more committee and subcommittee chairs for junior members, thus redistributing power. New rules were imposed for electing committee chairs and assigning members to committees. The procedures for hiring staff were also liberalized.

In 1946 Congress authorized staff for all its subcommittees. They have been growing in number, quality, and professionalism ever since. Some observers feel the staff is too influential in the policy-making process.[4] Whether they are or not, one must remember that Capitol Hill staff serve at the pleasure of the member for whom they work. They have no civil service protection, no seniority provisions, and no appeals process for dismissals. When staff members speak, one can be reasonably certain that their remarks reflect the views of the member of Congress who employs them.[5]

Just as legislators develop expertise by serving for a number of years on committees or subcommittees, so do staff members who work on these committees. But staff members work full time on their legislative and program concerns, whereas members are distracted by reelection campaigns, constituent service, party issues, travel, and other assignments.

Some of the functions performed by staff members include: organizing hearings by identifying witnesses and setting times and dates; conducting research on the issues confronting the committee; drafting bills and amendments; preparing committee reports; helping members prepare for floor debate; acting as a liaison with interest groups; and occasionally working in reelection campaigns. Committee staff members are characterized by limited advocacy and partisanship, loyalty to the chair (less true for those assigned to minority members), anonymity, and program specialization.[6]

Relationships between Congress and the bureaucracy are sometimes pictured as stormy hearings where representatives and senators sharply cross-examine cowed bureaucrats. These flamboyant, televised hearings are rare exceptions rather than the rule. Most hearings are quiet, with few people in attendance. Often only one subcommittee member represents the entire committee. People from all walks of life testify as witnesses.

Agency officials and committee staff members are in constant contact, making many policy decisions in a spirit of cooperation and compromise. When deadlocks occur, bureaucrats, committee staff members, and interested lobbyists must be able to bargain and negotiate in good faith if the debated issue is going to move forward. Failure to achieve a negotiated compromise means the issue will die, an outcome most participants in the process do not want.

The legislative branch oversees the bureaucracy in routine, quiet ways. Congress is responsible for passing and implementing legislation and for the impact programs have on society. The latter is an oversight function exercised by the congressional subcommittees.

They evaluate the performance of agency or bureau personnel when their programs are due for reauthorization and annually when funds are appropriated for programs.

With hundreds of programs, numerous bureaus and agencies, millions of employees, and billions of dollars being spent by the executive branch, the effectiveness of congressional oversight is necessarily limited. No legislative body could be organized enough to work on legislation, satisfy constituent requests, and then monitor the federal bureaucracy, all with equal effectiveness. Moreover, there are few incentives for members of Congress to pursue oversight activites; they are time-consuming and usually do not enhance reelection chances.

In an effort to ensure more effective oversight of the administration of federal programs, congressional committees employ a variety of strategies. Some legislation mandates periodic evaluations of the program, with regular reports submitted to the appropriate committee for review. These evaluations may be performed by outside third parties such as consultants, by state or local government agencies administering the programs, or by federal agency personnel. Whoever the evaluator is, Congress is assured of receiving information about a program it has funded.

One of the most effective oversight mechanisms is the appropriations process. When there is doubt about a program's value or concern about its direction, Congress can always cut the amount of money appropriated for it. Over the past eight years, for example, Congress has used this tactic to reduce the funds available to the Department of Housing and Urban Development for policy research. More recently it has cut the funding available to the District of Columbia for consultant services.

To assist in its oversight and investigative functions, Congress also uses the Office of Technology Assessment, the Congressional Research Service, the Congressional Budget Office, and the General Accounting Office. All of these offices conduct hundreds of studies each year at the request of committee members seeking to monitor and evaluate programs of interest to them.[7]

The greatest obstacle to effective congressional oversight is the difficulty of devising measurable objectives for human services and social programs. Given the problems of developing firm and uniform standards, it is understandable why governmental oversight and auditing procedures can be so controversial.[8]

Congress is the most colorful component of the decisionmaking system, and in some respects the most powerful. It is open to public scrutiny and watched closely by the press and lobbyists. It has a decentralized power structure, which tends to intensify debate and controversy. Congress is a collection of elected officials representing a great number of diverse interests—regional, economic, urban, ethnic, agricultural, banking, manufacturing, consumer, and senior citizens. Accommodating these constituencies requires skill and patience. But Congress does not work alone. Other institutions in the decisionmaking systems often challenge and compete with legislative goals.

## WASHINGTON LOBBYISTS

Interest groups, or lobbies, have a low reputation with the general public. Stereotypes often depict them engaging in covert, even illegal, activities and wielding undue influence in the policymaking process by means of bribes, illegal campaign contributions, and expensive gifts. Some unethical behavior undeniably occurs in both political and administrative life, but the overwhelming number of lobbyists in Washington do not participate in these influence-peddling activities.

The exact number of lobbyists in Washington is hard to determine. A *Time* magazine cover story in 1978 claimed that the number of lobbyists had increased from 8,000 to 15,000 in the previous five years. The largest growth area had been in representatives of major corporations. *Time* reported that more than 500 corporations supported Washington lobbies; that number was up from roughly 100 corporations ten years earlier.[9] More recent studies put the number of professional, full-time Washington lobbyists at around 7,000.[10] The *National Journal* claims that as many as 40,000 people engage in some form of lobbying at any given time. About 5,000 are registered with Congress.[11]

The right of the people to petition government is guaranteed by the First Amendment to the Constitution. This provision mandates minimal control of lobbying, because the right of private citizens to petition and present their views to government officials is fundamental to democratic government. Under great pressure to control lobbies, Congress inserted a section in the Legislative Reorganization

Act of 1946 requiring that groups spending money principally for the purpose of influencing legislation must register with the clerk of the House and the secretary of the Senate and also file quarterly financial statements. (See Appendix D for information on registering as a lobbyist.) The amount spent by each group is now public information. *Congressional Quarterly* publishes in every issue a list of the groups spending the most on lobbying and how much they spent. A complete list is published in the *Congressional Record.*

Individuals and organizations engaged in lobbying must keep detailed records of all contributions they receive, including names and addresses of all contributors of over $500. A record must also be kept of all expenditures made by or on behalf of the organization and of the names and addresses of payees. The law requires that written receipts be kept for at least two years after a lobbying group registers with Congress.

The penalty for violating these rules is a fine of not more than $5,000, or imprisonment for not more than one year, or both. Persons convicted of such violations may not attempt to influence the passage or defeat of any legislation for a period of three years. The penalty for committing this resulting felony is a fine of not more than $10,000, imprisonment for not more than five years, or both.[12] The registration law has proved difficult to enforce, however, because the scope of activity it covers is difficult to define precisely. Furthermore, most lobbyists do not spend all or even most of their time lobbying. They educate, write, do research, plan strategy, discuss, and transmit information between government decisionmaking systems and their employers.

Lobbying is a standard democratic practice protected by the First Amendment; consequently, it is difficult to regulate by federal legislation. Some state governments have enacted even stricter lobbying rules. In a few states even those who sell to government must register as lobbyists. This is an uncertain area of the law and susceptible to challenge. Thus far, federal law does not impose a single standard for who must register as a lobbyist and what must be reported. As a result, lobbyists receive vastly different treatment from all the governmental units in this country.[13]

There is also widespread disagreement about the effectiveness of the registration requirement as a control mechanism. It is difficult to determine if the filed reports of lobbyists are complete and accurate. In Washington the reports are almost never audited or investigated.

In fact, some claim that the lobby registration requirements are too weak to regulate lobbying effectively. The unintentional result of the regulations is the certification of a new profession. Lawyers, public relations specialists, and other free-lance entrepreneurs can register, then promote themselves to both small businesses and large corporations as a "Registered Lobbyist, Congress of the United States." This is a quick and easy way to establish credentials that attract a clientele. The development of this new profession is one of the ironies of the attempt to control a function so basic to democracy; the right of all citizens to petition their government.

### The Intermediary Role of Lobbyists

Interest groups can be categorized in many different ways. There are large groups representing general areas like labor, religion, agriculture, and business. Other interest groups act on behalf of narrower concerns, focusing perhaps on ethnic or minority issues, defense spending or weaponry, environmental concerns, or issues of interest to foreign governments. Professional associations for social workers, doctors, educators, and many others are located in Washington where they can influence policymakers on issues relevant to their members. There are also organizations representing veterans, children, the handicapped, gays, motorcyclists, airline pilots, and marijuana smokers.[14]

Whatever their purpose or scope may be, these groups all have one thing in common: access to the decisionmaking system. The decisionmaking system is deliberative, with many checks and balances. Experienced lobbyists know the numerous points in the process where legislation unfavorable to their clients can be stalled, modified, or defeated.

Lobbyists use a variety of techniques, depending upon the issue, who is in support or opposition, public opinion, upcoming elections, the position of the president, and many other factors. Some of the most common techniques are: contacting members of the decisionmaking system; encouraging influential constituents to pressure members of Congress; promoting their position through mail campaigns; and providing money, staff, or other services in an election campaign.[15]

Lobbyists spend most of their time in defensive "fire fighting" activities, like trying to convince a representative that a proposed amendment is expensive, inconsequential, or detrimental to the national interest. They might suggest funding cutbacks to an appropriations subcommittee staff member, or recommend word changes in the rules and regulations for a new program. Lobbyists work primarily with members of Congress and their staffs, reinforcing belief in their own positions. A lobbyist's time is much better spent building trust among the faithful than in trying to make converts.

Information is an interest group's greatest asset for swaying staff members and elected representatives. Lobbyists use specialists and other resources to gather accurate information on the issues under debate. Information gives lobbyists access to policymakers, many of whom seek out lobbyists for briefings on issues of current legislative interest.

Lobbyists who understand the decisionmaking system appreciate the importance of the bureaucrat's role, and will also spend time with mid-level agency personnel in bargaining and negotiating for their interest group's position. Lobbyists check in with bureaucrats to learn what the legislative agenda is and how they can influence it. Placement and timing of an issue on the legislative agenda are often the most important factors, for Congress has more issues before it than it has time to deal with them. Lobbyists therefore try to give bureaucrats critical information before the agenda-setting meetings.

Lobbyists and agency personnel occasionally rely upon each other to exert pressure on people in congressional offices. When a direct approach might be imprudent or ineffective, one will ask the other to talk with a personal friend of a committee staff member. Such favors carry the full understanding that they will be reciprocated at a later date.[16]

Despite the complaints from Congress about the unhealthy influence of special interest groups, legislators have followed the same basic pattern by establishing informal groups, or caucuses. Some caucuses are partisan, like the Democratic Study Group and the House Republican Study Committee. Others operate in only one house or the other, such as the Local Government Caucus in the House and the Drug Enforcement Caucus in the Senate. But most caucuses are bipartisan, include members from both houses, and represent very specialized interests like coal, steel, space, wine, mushrooms, senior citizens, water, jewelry, and automobiles. Members who are interested in any such issues will usually join the appropriate caucus. When legislation of interest to the caucus comes before a congressional committee, the caucus will select one of its members to be an early witness and present the views of the caucus to the committee. In a political system that values bargaining and reciprocity, a colleague's testimony can be crucial to the outcome of the legislation.[17]

It is difficult to assess the impact of the caucuses. Over the last fifteen years they have grown in number and influence. Some members say that they duplicate the work of other congressional offices and that they waste space, staff, and resources. Others point to the decline of the political parties and view congressional caucuses as a contributor to that decline. Nevertheless, it has at times been clear that the caucuses were responsible for the passage of important legislation.

To be successful in the policymaking process, lobbyists develop and use a number of access points. In addition to influencing the authorization and appropriation processes in Congress, lobbyists attempt to sway decisionmakers in the Office of Management and Budget as well as the Domestic Policy Council staff in the White House and the special assistants to the president.

Not all lobbyist-bureaucrat interaction takes place when legislation is being developed. Once legislation is passed, bureaucrats are responsible for drafting rules and regulations to guide the implementation process. Lobbyists know that these decisions made after passage can often be as important as the earlier decisions of the legislative drafting stage. By monitoring agency activities after a bill is signed into law, lobbyists can ensure that their constituents' views are well represented in the new administrative guidelines.[18]

### Resources of Lobbyists

A lobbyist's information is often more important in the long run than negotiating skills or special access to members, but the information must be reasonably accurate. Bureaucrats, committee staff, elected officials, and White House personnel frequently use this information in formulating policy proposals or in making decisions about pending legislation. A lobbyist trying to establish credibility within a particular decisionmaking system cannot afford to give that system false or misleading information. Many other interest groups are competing sources of information. Misleading data is often quickly exposed by other lobbyists and those misled become skeptical of the purveyors of such information. Credibility is essential to a lobbyist; without it there is no access, and without access a lobbyist is ineffective.

Several other factors contribute to the success or failure of interest groups. One is the proper allocation of the amount of influence an interest group possesses. If a group uses all of its resources on one issue, it is likely to find itself unable to affect decisions on issues that arise later. An interest group must plan its strategy on each issue so as to maximize the impact of its limited resources, thereby retaining enough in reserve to cope with future issues.

Knowing how to expend resources is one factor, and knowing when to use them is another. Resources used too early are wasted and lost forever. But resources that are held back too long, until after the important decisions have been made, will have had no effect on the outcome. Interest groups try to minimize timing errors by constantly monitoring the daily activities of the relevant decisionmaking systems. They try to learn what all the participants are thinking and which issues are scheduled for final debate and decision. All the interest groups thus gain the opportunity to plan their campaigns for participating in the debates and influencing the final decision.

Few interest groups have the time, money, or staff to wage a long and expensive campaign for or against an issue. To minimize their risks and to increase their clout, many interest groups form coalitions and pool their resources. Coordinating the strategy for diverse groups is not an easy task, but the anticipated impact on the system outweighs the organizational headaches. On some issues coalitions make for strange bedfellows. Labor and business, which oppose each other regularly, have joined forces on key votes in Congress on the Vietnam War and wage and price controls. In politics today's enemy can be tomorrow's ally; interest groups rarely develop a network of permanent allies because different issues demand different strategies.[19]

The typical lobbyist watches decisionmaking processes closely and tells allies and supporters when and where issues will be discussed or voted on. A lobbyist will even inform members of Congress of the moment a crucial vote (for the lobbyist) is about to be taken in committee. Sometimes lobbyists arrange for a member of Congress to receive a timely call from another member, the White House, other lobbyists, or important constituents. The expert lobbyist has a highly developed sense of what should be said to whom, by whom, and when. Skillfully bringing together the forces in the decisionmaking systems is the lobbyist's important contribution to government.

## BUSINESS POLITICAL ACTION COMMITTEES

A 1971 change in the campaign financing laws gave corporations and business associations a chance to participate more directly in political and electoral processes through Political Action Committees (PACs). PACs raise funds from corporate employees and stockholders to use as contributions to political campaigns and political parties. (How to organize a corporate PAC is explained in Appendix E.)

PACs emerged in the 1940s as a union initiative after the Smith–Connally Act of 1943 made it illegal for unions to use dues for campaign contributions. Created by the unions as separate organizations, the early PACs collected dues on their own from union members to support candidates favored by the unions. The largest, created in 1955 by the AFL–CIO, is the Committee on Political Education (COPE).

Business did not follow the lead of the unions. There were some PACs for small businesses, but most contributions were made individually by leading members of the business community. (It is illegal to donate directly from corporate treasuries.) The earliest corporate PAC with any influence was BIPAC, the Business Industrial Political Action Committee. Founded by the National Association of Manufacturers in the 1960s, it was similar to COPE in its organization. Business started seriously organizing PACs in the 1970s.

There are two reasons why PACs became more feasible and attractive to business. One was a change in the federal election laws that put greater restrictions on the amount of money an individual could give to a candidate or political party. This change occurred after the Watergate scandals had prompted public scrutiny of violations in corporate giving practices. The second catalyst was the Federal Election Campaign Act of 1971, which specifically sanctioned corporate PACs. One obstacle remained; the 1971 act still prohibited organizations with government contracts from organizing Political Action Committees. A 1974 amendment to the act eliminated that

Table 6-1.  Largest PAC Contributors, 1983–84 Elections.

| | |
|---|---|
| National Conservative Political Action Committee | $19.3 |
| Fund for a Conservative Majority | 5.5 |
| National Congressional Club | 5.2 |
| Realtors Political Action Club | 3.9 |
| National Rifle Association Political Victory Fund | 3.8 |
| Republican Majority Fund | 3.5 |
| American Medical Association PAC | 3.5 |
| Ruff PAC | 3.5 |
| Fund for a Democratic Majority | 3.0 |
| Citizens for the Republic | 2.8 |
| National Committee to Preserve Social Security PAC | 2.4 |
| National Committee for an Effective Congress | 2.4 |
| Campaign for Prosperity | 2.2 |
| National Education Association PAC | 2.2 |
| National PAC | 2.1 |

Source: *National Journal*, June 15, 1985, p. 1429.

barrier. These changes in the federal election laws led to an explosion in the number of corporate PACs, from about 450 in 1976 to 1,700 in 1985.[20]

In 1983–84 PACs spent $112.6 million on congressional and presidential candidates; fifteen PACs spent over 60 percent of the total. Democrats received about $64 million and Republicans $49 million. Table 6-1 shows the largest contributions.

PACs are allowed to solicit contributions from employees, and some corporations even use payroll withholding plans for contributions. Employees are often asked to indicate their favored candidate or party. A corporate committee then decides where to contribute unearmarked funds. Changes in campaign finance laws have created greater flexibility for PACs than for individual givers. An individual can contribute only $1,000 per election to any candidate, with a $25,000 annual limit. Individuals also may give up to $20,000 to the national party committee and as much as $5,000 to other political committees, but the annual limit is still $25,000. PACs, on the other hand, may give $5,000 per election to any candidate, with no annual limit on total contributions. Furthermore, PACs may contribute $15,000 a year to a national party committee and $5,000 to other election committees.

Most candidates' funds still come primarily from individual donors, but the dollar impact of PACs is growing more substantial every year. In the 1978 congressional campaigns, 18 percent of the $199 million spent by candidates came from PACs. By 1982 that figure had exceeded 25 percent, with PACs contributing nearly 29 percent of House campaign funds and nearly 15 percent in Senate races.[21] The rising importance of PACs has generated demands for public financing of congressional elections. Since 1976 the presidential campaigns have been financed in part through public funds. As PACs become more influential, efforts will probably intensify to mitigate their importance and put more of the burden for congressional campaign funds on the public treasury.

### Questions of PAC Effectiveness and Reform

PACs are important mechanisms for corporate support of political candidates, but their effectiveness in influencing candidates has not been determined. Even their impact on the two major parties is not entirely clear. Corporate and other business-related PACs favored Democratic *incumbents* over Republican *challengers* by a margin of more than two to one in the 1976 general elections. This is partly because more Democratic than Republican incumbents were running for reelection. The Republican party, however, profited more overall from corporate PACs. Corporate PACs directed 59 percent of their contributions to Republican candidates, while nearly 97 percent of union PAC contributions went to Democrats.

PAC contributions have not always swayed a recipient toward the donor's point of view. The House passed a tax reform proposal in late 1985 that was opposed by business PACs, yet many business PAC beneficiaries voted for it. A lobbyist for the National Realty Committee called the House bill "abominable." Referring to PAC contributions, he observed, "If your motive is to influence public policy, then there's a lot of money being wasted."[22]

Yet the growing strength and visibility of PACs has generated great concern in many quarters. Senate Majority Leader, Robert Dole of Kansas, said, "When these PACs give money, they expect something in return other than good government." PAC representatives are particularly visible on major issues like tax reform. According to former Senator Gary Hart of Colorado, "What the public perceives is, quite bluntly, bribery."[23]

As campaign expenses grow, PAC support will undoubtedly continue to be important to candidates. But the influence of money on politics raises serious questions in a representative system of government. Proposals to limit PAC contributions or otherwise restrict their power will probably become law in the next few years, but such efforts are not likely to be very effective. Public support of political campaigns through the U.S. Treasury Department may appear to some as the most effective way of dismantling the power of special interest contributors. Government support, however, raises other problems. There is some evidence that the business community might want to limit PACs and support government financing of campaigns. John Albertine, past president of the American Business Conference, says, "The whole thing is getting out of hand, and it's so bad, that it's not good for business. There's enormous pressure on business to contribute to all sorts of campaigns, and the pressure to contribute far exceeds the ability to do so."[24] Debate over the equity of an electoral system so heavily influenced by PACs, and questions on how to reform that system, are likely to be around for some time. These new complaints from business about the high cost of political campaigns could accelerate the movement for reform.

Business lobbying in Washington is a lively activity. The decision-making systems of government are open to corporate participation. The participation of business is sought after and welcomed as long as the rules of the game are followed. Working effectively within the decision systems is a management skill expected of the corporate executive today.

## NOTES

1. The approaches to government decisionmaking elaborated upon in this chapter are discussed at greater length in Ernest S. Griffith, *Congress: Its Contemporary Role* (New York: New York University Press, 1961); Douglas Cater, *Power in Washington* (New York: Random House, 1964); J. Leiper Freeman, *The Political Process*, rev. ed. (New York: Random House, 1965); and A. Lee Fritschler, *Smoking and Politics: Policymaking and the Federal Bureaucracy*, 3d ed. (Englewood Cliffs, N.J.: Prentice-Hall, 1983).

2. See Randall B. Ripley, *Congress: Process and Policy*, 3d ed. (New York: W. W. Norton, 1983), pp. 199–201, for an analysis of committee and floor votes in Congress over several years.

3.  For a more detailed discussion of the role of party leaders, see Ripley, *Congress*, ch. 6. See also Roger H. Davidson and Walter J. Oleszek, *Congress and Its Members*, 2d ed. (Washington, D.C.: Congressional Quarterly Press, 1985), ch. 7.

4.  See Michael J. Malbin, "Congressional Committee Staffs: Who's in Charge Here?" *The Public Interest* 47 (Spring 1977): 16–40. Two recent studies are Steven S. Smith and Christopher J. Deering, *Committees in Congress* (Washington, D.C.: Congressional Quarterly Press, 1984), ch. 7, and Michael J. Malbin, *Unelected Representatives: Congressional Staff and the Future of Representative Government* (New York: Basic Books, 1980).

5.  For a useful and interesting analysis of congressional staff, see Harrison E. Fox, Jr. and Susan Webb Hammond, *Congressional Staff: The Invisible Force in American Lawmaking* (New York: The Free Press, 1975). See also Davidson and Oleszek, *Congress and Its Members*, ch. 9, and Smith and Deering, *Committees in Congress*, ch. 7.

6.  Ripley, *Congress*, pp. 260–76.

7.  For a critical discussion of the functions of these agencies, see James A. Thurber, "Policy Analysis of Capitol Hill: Issues Facing the Four Analytical Support Agencies of Congress," *Policy Studies Journal* 6 (Autumn 1977): 101–11. See also Davidson and Oleszek, *Congress and Its Members*, pp. 255–57, 428–29.

8.  For a discussion of the techniques and limitations of congressional oversight, see Walter J. Oleszek, *Congressional Procedures and the Policy Process* (Washington, D.C.: Congressional Quarterly Press, 1978), pp. 202–12. See also Davidson and Oleszek, *Congress and Its Members*, pp. 340–42, and Randall B. Ripley and Grace A. Franklin, *Congress, the Bureaucracy, and Public Policy*, 3d ed. (Homewood, Ill.: Dorsey Press, 1984), pp. 19–21, 67–69, 248–56.

9.  "The Swarming Lobbyists," *Time*, 7 August 1978.

10. An examination of the Washington lobbying community can be found in Kay Lehman Schlozman and John T. Tierney, *Organized Interests and American Democracy* (New York: Harper and Row, 1986), pp. 63–82. See also Jeffrey M. Berry, *The Interest Group Society* (Boston: Little, Brown, 1984), pp. 18–26.

11. Burt Solomon, "How Washington Works," *National Journal* 18 (1986): 1426–32.

12. Details of the law can be found in the Legislative Reorganization Act of 1946 (Public Law 601; 2 U.S.C. 261–270). See also *Federal Regulation of Lobbying Act: Outline of Instructions for Filing Reports* (Washington, D.C.: U.S. Government Printing Office, 1976).

13. For a discussion of lobbying history and some current efforts to expand the regulation of lobbyists, see Norman J. Ornstein and Shirley Elder, *Interest Groups, Lobbying and Policymaking* (Washington, D.C.: Congres-

sional Quarterly Press, 1978), pp. 101–14. See also Berry, *The Interest Group Society*, pp. 214–217, and Schlozman and Tierney, *Organized Interests and American Democracy*, pp. 317–21.

14.   One interesting way of classifying interest groups is used by Lewis Anthony Dexter in *How Organizations Are Represented in Washington* (Indianapolis: Bobbs-Merrill, 1969), ch. 2. Another typology of interest groups can be found in Ornstein and Elder, *Interest Groups*, pp. 35–53. See also Berry, *The Interest Group Society*, ch. 2, and Schlozman and Tierney, *Organized Interests and American Democracy*, ch. 3.

15.   For a discussion of lobbying techniques, see Carol S. Greenwald, *Group Power: Lobbying and Public Policy* (New York: Praeger, 1977), pp. 68–84. See also Berry, *The Interest Group Society*, pp. 99–113, and Schlozman and Tierney, *Organized Interests and American Democracy*, chs. 7 and 12.

16.   For more detail, see Schlozman and Tierney, *Organized Interest Groups and American Democracy*, ch. 11.

17.   Davidson and Oleszek, *Congress and Its Members*, pp. 362–68. See also Susan Webb Hammond, Arthur Stevens, Jr., and Daniel P. Mulhollan, "Congressional Caucuses: Legislators as Lobbyists," in Allan J. Cigler and Burdett A. Loomis, eds., *Interest Group Politics* (Washington, D.C.: Congressional Quarterly Press, 1983), pp. 275–97.

18.   See Schlozman and Tierney, *Organized Interest Groups and American Democracy*, pp. 330–353.

19.   See ibid., ch. 5, and Berry, *The Interest Group Society*, pp. 110–113.

20.   Federal Election Commission, Press Release, July 14, 1986.

21.   Federal Elections Commission, *The First Ten Years, 1975–85*, April 1985.

22.   Quoted in Brooks Jackson, "Ways and Means Measure Puts Biggest Tax Bites on Some of the Most Prolific Campaign Donors," *Wall Street Journal*, 11 December 1985.

23.   Both quoted in "Special Interest Snipers," *New York Times*, 21 November 1985.

24.   Quoted in David Shibman and Brooks Jackson, "Conservative Support Adds Momentum to a Move by Congress to Limit PAC's Influence in Elections," *Wall Street Journal*, 22 November 1985.

# 7 MANAGING THE DECISIONMAKING SYSTEMS
## Administrative Agencies and the Executive Office of the President

Power is distributed unevenly in government decisionmaking systems. Members of Congress, members of the White House staff, and the Washington lobbyists are all active and important, but the administrative agencies have powerful advantages over all other participants. The managers of the administrative agencies orchestrate the decisionmaking systems and are usually more responsible than others for the success or failure of government programs.

Successful agency leadership depends on cultivating good relations with everyone involved in the system and, to a lesser extent, with the media and the public. The agencies have the crucial responsibility of knowing what changes can be made, how quickly, and how to activate the momentum necessary to keep a program moving through both legislative and operational processing. To accomplish all this, administrative agencies rely on their bureaucratic expertise, relative longevity, institutional memory, and rulemaking authority delegated to them by Congress.

Expert knowledge is most highly concentrated in the bureaucracy. The bureaucracy attracts people with interest and commitment to the programs it administers. There are strong connections between agency leaders and the interest groups monitoring their programs. As discussed earlier, these relationships keep program information flowing into the agencies. Consequently, agencies almost always enjoy technical superiority over others in the decisionmaking system.

93

The bureaucracy enhances its expertise by compartmentalizing into small, manageable areas of specialization. Agency employees can thus concentrate on their field of expertise. Members of Congress must run for reelection and respond to their various constituencies; lobbyists often work on a broad range of programs. Without most of these outside distractions, agencies are better organized for specialization than Congress or the interest groups. Furthermore, the agencies are large enough to have adequate staff for the work on specific policy problems.[1]

Memory and access to information are important sources of power. The people working in agencies have usually been with the government for many years, or have private-sector experience with the programs they now manage. This long experience with an issue gives the bureaucrat extra leverage in decisionmaking and contributes to successful program management. Too much experience in one area, however, can also make it difficult for a bureaucrat to coordinate similar or competing government programs.

Those participating in government look to the bureaucracy for information about existing programs and plans for future ones. Agencies enhance their decisionmaking power by imparting information selectively and closely timing its release. Some agencies regularly deliver critical information to friendly legislators at just the right moment. Press releases can be timed to aid key legislators while hindering others. Wise bureaucrats use their positions to learn what everyone else is doing and what is needed to advance their own positions.[2]

Since bureaucrats possess both expertise and information, it is not surprising that elected officials seek their advice in making decisions in many areas, including drafting of legislation, preparation of budget requests, and preparation of testimony before congressional committee hearings. The most important agency powers, however, stem from their rulemaking authority delegated by Congress. This authority enables the agencies to interpret, shape, and even create the law. Increasingly, business executives are paying attention to the administrative agencies, because some of the most important decisions affecting business are made by bureaucrats through agency rulemaking activities.[3]

## RULEMAKING IN ADMINISTRATIVE AGENCIES

The dynamics of modern policymaking have expanded the role of bureaucracies. Democratic theory as well as the Constitution clearly stipulate that laws and policy should be made by Congress, with presidential concurrence, but the system has not worked quite that way for years. Almost from the beginning, Congress found it necessary to delegate lawmaking and policymaking powers to administrative agencies, which have the time and expertise to develop the rules and regulations necessary for administering legislated programs.[4] Congress gives agencies substantial power to write these rules and regulations that interpret, clarify, and implement its legislative intent. Thus most government rules and regulations are issued by the executive branch operating under delegation of authority from Congress.

One can better understand this policymaking process by looking at its three consecutive stages. The first stage is legislative; Congress passes a bill and the president signs it into law. The next two stages are administrative. An administrative agency clarifies the law and prepares it for implementation. Then the agency administers the law and in doing so the law is interpreted, elaborated, evaluated, and then reinterpreted. Rulemaking is a continual process.

The second and third stages are especially important. Usually Congress drafts laws in broad terms. Legislation can be vague and fraught with ambiguities spawned by political compromise. The administrative agencies must make the law operational by eliminating these ambiguities and developing well-defined procedures for implementation. Sometimes a law takes a different direction as a result of agency rulemaking activities. This is why business executives should carefully observe this stage of the policymaking process. The stages of agency rulemaking are illustrated in Figure 7-1.

Looking at the legislation that created the Federal Communications Commission (FCC) can illuminate the process of congressional delegation to an agency. The legislation was passed in 1934 and is very brief. Congress simply created the commission, authorized the number of commissioners to be appointed, and described generally the commission's jurisdiction. The "operational" part of the legislation was a plain statement that the FCC should regulate U.S. wireless communications for the "public interest, convenience and necessity." Under that broad delegation of authority, the commission decided myriad questions about the regulation of the radio, television, and telecommunications industries. The FCC has written thousands of rules and regulations on the technicalities of this area as well as on related social and political ramifications.

Every federal agency has such powers delegated to it by Congress. The Department of Agriculture has great influence over the agricul-

**Figure 7-1.** Know Your Federal Regulations.

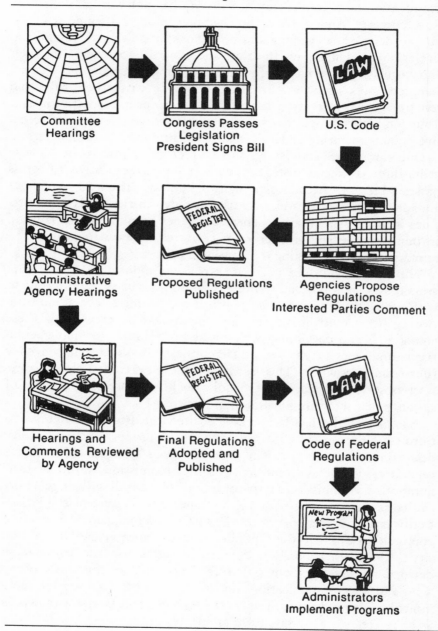

Committee Hearings

Congress Passes Legislation President Signs Bill

U.S. Code

Administrative Agency Hearings

Proposed Regulations Published

Agencies Propose Regulations Interested Parties Comment

Hearings and Comments Reviewed by Agency

Final Regulations Adopted and Published

Code of Federal Regulations

Administrators Implement Programs

Source: National Association of Counties, Washington, D.C.

tural sector of the economy through its powers to write rules and regulations in this program area. The Internal Revenue Service has broad discretionary powers to write rules and regulations that affect all of us.

Because this delegated authority is such a powerful tool, and the Constitution does clearly place lawmaking authority in the legislative branch, Congress strives to responsibly oversee the administrative policymaking process. These efforts are made to protect our constitutional rights. In 1946 Congress passed the Administrative Procedure Act, which outlines certain requirements for administrative agencies in their rulemaking procedures. For example, agencies must publish in the *Federal Register* any proposed changes in existing rules and regulations and proposals for new ones. Agencies must accept the written comments of interested parties on rule changes or new rules being considered. Sometimes the agencies hold hearings and invite testimony. These procedures ensure that public views will be heard while agencies are drafting rules and regulations. (For more information on the *Federal Register*, see Appendix B.)

## HEARINGS IN THE AGENCIES

When an administrative agency is making rules, its hearings are similar to those of the congressional committees. Hearing rooms in administrative agencies look like the ones on Capitol Hill, familiar to anyone who has seen televised hearings. The agency hearings are presided over by agency staff members or sometimes by the agency directors. Regulatory commission hearings are run by the commissioners themselves. Witnesses submit written testimony ahead of time, state their positions orally at the hearing, and then answer questions posed by the hearing officers. The agency keeps transcripts of the hearings to use in reaching a decision. Anyone who wants to testify may do so simply by notifying the clerk of the agency. If many people want to testify, oral testimony time may be limited; but the agencies seldom place limits on the amount of written testimony they will accept.

Agencies also have quasi-judicial powers. They have some authority to resolve conflicts between individuals or between individuals and the government. Resolving disputes over the awarding of licenses is one example of this type of activity. The agencies may also hold hearings on violations of rules and regulations by either corporations or individuals, where a finding in favor of the government could result in the imposition of a fine or other penalty.

These quasi-judicial hearings are presided over by administrative law judges and operate under procedures similar to those in a regular court of law. These agency judges are an elite corps of civil servants recruited through competitive examinations. The validity of these administrative processes is largely dependent on their integrity, just as the validity of the judicial system rests on the integrity of its judges.

The rules and decisions of administrative agencies can almost always be appealed to the judicial courts. The courts, however, are sometimes reluctant to review decisions, recognizing that they are based on the agency's expertise. They generally confine their involvement to review of questions on agency procedures, authority, or jurisdiction. If an agency has violated due process of law in its hearing procedures, the courts may overturn the decision. In doing so, the courts generally will not decide on the merits of the case, but simply remand the decision back to the agency for another hearing, with instructions that this time the hearing is to be conducted properly.

After an agency adopts a rule, it is published in the *Code of Federal Regulations.*[5] The *Code* is fully indexed by agency or major program; it therefore contains all the rules and regulations that any given agency has promulgated or adopted. All amendments to the rules and regulations are also included in the *Code.* (See Appendix C for a description of the *Code of Federal Regulations.*)

A key publication for understanding the role of agencies, and one of enormous importance to business, is the *Federal Register.* The *Register* brought some order to the administrative chaos that existed before its first publication in 1936. Before then, there was no single document that contained all the official actions of agencies, including proposed rules, adopted rules, hearing notices, and application forms. Consequently, the government was unable to give out information to the public about administrators' actions except through mimeographed announcements, the press, and selected mailing lists. Congress created the *Federal Register* to end the inherent injustice in so haphazard a distribution of crucial government information.

The *Register* is published daily and has several thousand subscribers. Another few thousand copies are distributed free of charge.

All proposed changes in agency rules, regulations, and forms are announced in the *Register*, as are time limits for the submission of written comments on these rules and regulations. Final decisions of the agencies are also printed in the *Register* before they are entered in the *Code of Federal Regulations.*[6]

These delegated powers from Congress make administrative agencies central to the policymaking process. Congress can, and sometimes does, overrule agencies. Furthermore, the decisionmaking system operates in such a way that Congress knows bureaucrats will take the views of members into consideration at all times. Members of Congress even testify sometimes at agency rulemaking hearings. Nevertheless, agencies have a considerable advantage in the policymaking process because of their permanence, their expertise, and their access to records. The legal authority to write rules and regulations further enhances their decisionmaking power.

One device employed by Congress to monitor how the executive branch agencies use their delegated powers is the legislative veto. The legislative veto was first used in the 1930s to reconcile conflicting policy views. At first, the legislative veto allowed the president, regulatory agencies, and other government departments to propose rules and regulations that would go into effect unless overturned by either house or, in some cases, both houses. This procedure slowly evolved to the point where Congress had to approve, not disapprove, the proposed rules. In some cases congressional committees could challenge executive branch actions by exercising the legislative veto.

The legislative veto shortcuts the legislative process by allowing either house or a specific committee to veto rules and regulations written by an administrative agency. Supporters of the legislative veto have argued that it is a device for monitoring and controlling bureaucratic behavior. They see it as an essential tool for a legislative body attempting to stay abreast of government programs. Opponents see it as a device that enables Congress to meddle in the affairs of the executive branch. They argue that Congress delegated power to the bureaucracy by statute and cannot call it back by the action of one house or one congressional committee. Opponents also argue that the legislative veto can slow the policymaking processes enough to affect adversely all those concerned.

Since 1932 about 400 legislative veto provisions have been enacted—almost 300 of them since 1970. Eighty-seven legislative veto actions were passed in 1974–75, apparently in reaction to the abuses of executive power uncovered in the Watergate hearings. Up to 1983 Congress had passed 226 of 1,180 proposed veto resolutions, but it should be noted that less than 20 of those nullified a regulation proposed by an agency.[7]

In 1983 the Supreme Court ruled in the *Chadha* case that it was unconstitutional for Congress to veto rules and regulations issued by the executive branch. Congress can now exercise its veto power only if both houses approve the action and the president also signs the measure.[8] In response, Congress is trying to fashion a legislative veto bill that will meet the new standards established by the Court. Meanwhile, recent veto efforts have been directed at rules issued by the Federal Trade Commission and the Consumer Product Safety Commission.[9]

The legislative veto issue is just one sign of the constant tension between the agencies and congressional committees over the question of delegated powers. This tension, and the vigilance it generates, is healthy and guarantees that the voices of elected officials are heard clearly in the halls of agency policymaking. In a technologically complex society where decisionmaking requires expertise, a balance of power must be maintained between experts and elected officials. The competitive interaction in our policymaking systems helps to achieve such a balance.

Lobbyists have recently begun to recognize the importance of agency activity. Traditionally, lobbyists devoted most of their energies to Capitol Hill. In fact, the term *lobbyist* came into usage because the interest group representatives often met with members of Congress in the lobbies immediately adjoining the House and Senate chambers. Modern lobbyists can still be found on the Hill, but increasingly they spend more time working in the agencies. This diversification of interest group activity further underscores the importance of administrative agencies in policymaking.

## THE EXECUTIVE OFFICE OF THE PRESIDENT

Although the president seldom is directly involved in the hundreds of government decisionmaking systems, members of his staff are often active participants. The top staff people are busy assisting the president on immediate and crucial matters of foreign and domestic policy. The atmosphere can be intense, unpredictable, and occasionally chaotic. But there are less visible, less pressured departments of the Executive Office of the President that link up with the decisionmaking systems.

The three units of the Executive Office that wield influence over the domestic decisionmaking system are the White House Office, the Domestic Policy Council, and the Office of Management and Budget. The rest of the Executive Office staff perform highly specialized tasks and are involved only in the decisionmaking systems related to their specialties.

The White House Office was established by the Reorganization Act of 1939. The staff is composed of personal advisors to the president and numbers between eighty and ninety people. Upon assuming office, each president seeks to shape the Executive Office staff to fit his needs, goals, and working style. The White House Office is one place where the president has the flexibility to blend loyalty and expertise in the people chosen to become close personal advisors.

To work in the White House Office, the president appoints a chief counsel, a press secretary, and a public relations officer. He also appoints special assistants in areas such as consumer affairs and minority, ethnic, and women's issues. Each special assistant is likely to have a deputy assistant and a small support staff. The White House Office staff is responsible for maintaining communication with Congress, heads of other executive departments and administrative agencies, the media, the public, and special interest groups. They are the president's eyes and ears outside the White House.

In July 1970 President Nixon implemented one of the recommendations of the Advisory Council on Executive Management (the Ash Commission) by creating the Domestic Council. Nixon felt that the institutional arrangement for handling domestic policy under his three immediate predecessors lacked continuity, clearly defined responsibilities, techniques for planning and reviewing actions, and mechanisms for follow-through. What he wanted was a system for handling domestic policy modeled on the National Security Council's handling of foreign policy. He needed a team of respected analysts to solve disputes and clarify policy options.[10]

President Nixon assigned the following responsibilities to the Domestic Council:

1. Formulate and coordinate domestic policy recommendations to the president;

2. Assess national needs and coordinate the establishment of national priorities;
3. Provide a rapid response to presidential needs for policy advice on critical domestic issues;
4. Provide continuous review of ongoing domestic programs from a public standpoint;
5. Operate through a series of ad hoc project committees that deal with either broad program areas or specific problems;
6. Utilize staff support from departmental or agency experts, or its own staff.

The associate and assistant directors of the council acted as project managers. Each would take responsibility for a few key issues, while the planning staff provided the general support and coordination. The issues handled by the Domestic Council usually reflect presidential priorities. How staff is deployed on the issues indicates where the president is willing to commit resources—in time, money, people, influence, and public leadership.

Under Presidents Nixon and Ford, the Domestic Council focused on planning and follow-through activities. It was a conduit for proposals coming into the White House. The staff clarified options for the president by developing arguments for and against each policy issue. These arguments included the recommendations of departmental and Executive Office staff as well as the comments of the Domestic Council.

Many Domestic Council ideas materialized in these presidents' State of the Union messages or in their special messages to Congress on the budget or specific legislation. The messages to Congress were usually accompanied by supporting data to explain the president's position, provided by the Domestic Council.

The follow-through activities of the Domestic Council included monitoring proposals as they progressed through Congress, working with Congress on legislative language, and making decisions on legislative tactics, including final compromises. The Domestic Council also provided the political perspective in annual budget reviews and took charge of analyzing and then communicating program results through the media, speeches, press conferences, and White House briefings. The council also analyzed public opinion polls and political information to determine reactions to the president's domestic policies and to uncover new issues and problems requiring attention.

The Carter administration found this domestic policy process too chaotic and inefficient for its working style. In mid-1977 an Executive Office reorganization plan was implemented to strengthen the role of the president's chief domestic policy advisors. The purpose of Carter's Domestic Policy Staff was to increase the president's control over the development of major domestic programs.[11]

President Reagan came into office in 1981 committed to a domestic policy system that would encompass both strategic planning and policy management. To achieve his goals, he created the Office of Policy Development (OPD), the cabinet councils, and the Office of Planning and Evaluation (OPE).

The OPD, a modification of Carter's Domestic Policy Staff, focused on developing policy through the cabinet councils. OPD served as the executive secretariat to the five original cabinet councils, providing staff support and overall coordination. As the cabinet councils developed and grew in importance, OPD took on even more of a staff role and less of a policy development role. By the summer of 1985 OPD staff had been reduced and reassigned to the new Office of Cabinet Affairs, which oversees both the Economic and Domestic Policy Councils and works closely with the National Security Council.

Shortly after taking office, President Reagan announced the creation of five cabinet councils: Economic Affairs, Commerce and Trade, Human Resources, National Resources and Environment, and Food and Agriculture. The sixth and seventh councils—Legal Policy, and Management and Administration—were announced later. The purpose of the cabinet council system was to provide the president, who serves as chair on each council, with a flexible policymaking system. The council system is innovative in two respects: cabinet members are expected to participate, and the work of each council cuts across departmental lines.

President Reagan reorganized the cabinet council system after his reelection. On April 11, 1985, he announced two new cabinet-level councils, the Economic Policy Council, headed by Treasury Secretary James Baker, and the Domestic Policy Council, headed by Attorney General Edwin Meese. These new cabinet councils replaced the existing five councils, perhaps signaling that White House Chief of Staff Donald T. Regan wanted a smaller, more orderly policymaking system at his disposal.

The cabinet councils do not always rubber-stamp policy presented to them. In mid-1985 Attorney General Edwin Meese proposed a modification in the executive order on affirmative action. Meese felt that the executive order was being interpreted as setting quotas for hiring, rather than goals. But Labor Secretary William Brock thought that those interpretations should be modified, not the wording of the executive order. Brock was supported by organized labor and many large businesses across the country, who thought satisfactory progress was being made under the current executive order. When the issue reached the agenda of the Domestic Policy Council, Brock was able to gather enough support to defer modifications in the executive order to a later date.

The Office of Planning and Evaluation had a smaller staff that worked primarily on the preparation of strategic planning documents related to the policy goals of the Reagan administration. Even though its evaluations were important, it was dissolved in 1985 because there was virtually no need for the work it was producing.[12]

## THE OFFICE OF MANAGEMENT AND BUDGET

The largest unit in the Executive Office of the President that has power to affect policy is the Office of Management and Budget. OMB was created by President Nixon in 1970 to free up the old Bureau of the Budget for more management responsibility.[13] Initially, the OMB director and deputy director were appointed by the president without congressional confirmation. Now these appointees must be confirmed by the Senate. The politically sensitive nature of the two positions has made them targets of controversy almost from the beginning.

OMB has a staff of around 600 professionals. Their major responsibility is to assist the president in preparing the budget and in formulating his fiscal program. They are also charged with control and administration of the budget. These responsibilities keep the OMB staff in constant communication with the agencies and other departments of government: first on budget questions, then on legislative issues, and finally on administrative matters.

OMB participates fully and regularly in the policymaking process. If a bureau head wants to initiate a new program or make substantial changes in an existing one—changes that require congressional action—the proposal must first have the written approval of OMB before it can move forward to Capitol Hill. This legislative clearance function combined with its regular budget functions, makes OMB perhaps the most powerful agency of government. Presidents rely heavily on OMB as they attempt to influence policy, control costs, or exercise control over government programs.

The OMB also works with the president to improve the efficiency of government services and coordination among agencies; to promote the better administrative management; to advise the president on legislation ready for his signature; to plan and implement the production of program performance data; and to conduct program evaluations.

As the president seeks to influence the outcome of hundreds of decisionmaking processes, he has at his disposal a personal staff of specialists, the cabinet councils, and his strongest asset, the OMB. This is an impressive array of resources, but on any given issue they will not assure the president of victory.[14]

Interest groups, Congress, and agency bureaucrats all have power in decisionmaking systems. Depending upon the degree of coordination, timing, resource commitment, and perseverance, any of these groups can stall or even defeat a presidential program. But they can also accelerate the process and move an issue quickly to a positive conclusion. The decisionmaking systems work as well as they do be because they are balanced. No one group dominates another unless there is a major national crisis. Short of that, all participants are working to achieve the best possible compromise consistent with stated goals and objectives.

## NOTES

1. See Francis E. Rourke, *Bureaucracy, Politics, and Public Policy*, 3d ed. (Boston: Little, Brown, 1984), pp. 15–20.

2. For a discussion of cooperation between program managers and members of Congress, see James A. Thurber, "The Actors in Administering Public Policy: Legislative Administrative Relations," *Policy Studies Journal* 5 (Autumn 1976): 56–65. Also see Randall B. Ripley and Grace A. Franklin, *Congress, The Bureaucracy, and Public Policy*, 3d ed. (Homewood, Ill.: Dorsey Press, 1984), ch. 3, and Roger H. Davidson and Walter J. Oleszek, *Congress and Its Members*, 2d ed. (Washington, D.C.: Congressional Quarterly Press, 1985), pp. 319–27.

3. See Ripley and Franklin, *Congress, the Bureaucracy, and Public Policy*, ch. 3, and Rourke, *Bureaucracy, Politics, and Public Policy*, ch. 2.

4.  For a discussion of the procedures and policymaking powers at administrative agencies, see A. Lee Fritschler, *Smoking and Politics: Policymaking and the Federal Bureaucracy*, 3d ed. (Englewood Cliffs, N.J.: Prentice–Hall, 1983), chs. 5 and 6.

5.  The *Code of Federal Regulations* is published by the Office of the Federal Register, National Archives and Records Services, General Service Administration, Washington, D.C.

6.  A comprehensive guide to the *Federal Register* can be found in *The Federal Register: What It Is and How to Use It* (Washington, D.C.: U.S. Government Printing Office, 1985).

7.  Stephen Labaton, "Legislative Veto Called Alive and Well," *Washington Post*, 7 August 1985.

8.  *Chadha v. Immigration and Naturalization Service*, 634 F.2d 408 433 (9th Cir. 1980). See also Laurence H. Tribe, "The Legislative Veto Decision: A Law By Any Other Name?" *Harvard Journal on Legislation* 21 (Winter 1984): 1–27.

9.  A good overview of some of the conflicts on this issue can be found in Louis Fisher, *Constitutional Conflicts Between Congress and the President* (Princeton, N.J.: Princeton University Press, 1985).

10. An analysis of the Domestic Council can be found in Raymond J. Waldmann, "The Domestic Council: Innovation in Presidential Government," *Public Administration Review* 36 (May–June 1976): 260–68. See also Dom Bonafede, "White House Staffing: The Nixon–Ford Era," in Thomas E. Cronin and Rexford G. Tugwell, eds., *The Presidency Reappraised*, 2d ed. (New York: Praeger, 1977), pp. 16–61, 169–70.

11. David Broder, "Shaping the Administration's Policy: New Process for Domestic Issues," *Washington Post*, 12 February 1978.

12. For a discussion of the inner workings of the Reagan White House staff, see Chester A. Newland, "The Reagan Presidency: Limited Government and Political Administration," *Public Administration Review* 43 (1983): 1–21. See also Dick Kirschten, "White House Notebook," *National Journal* 17 (1985): 1418–19, 1997, and Chester A. Newland, "Executive Office Policy Apparatus: Enforcing the Reagan Agenda," in Lester M. Salomon and Michael S. Lund, eds., *The Reagan Presidency and the Governing of America* (Washington, D.C.: Urban Institute Press, 1984).

13. For an analysis of the role of OMB in the political process, see Larry Beman, *The Office of Management and Budget and the Presidency, 1921–1979* (Princeton, N.J.: Princeton University Press, 1979). See also Frederick C. Mosher, *A Tale of Two Agencies* (Baton Rouge: Louisiana State University Press, 1984).

14. The classic study of the use of presidential influence remains Richard E. Neustadt, *Presidential Power: The Politics of Leadership from FDR to Carter* (New York: John Wiley and Sons, 1980).

# 8 THE DECISIONMAKING SYSTEMS IN OPERATION

The decisionmaking systems of government are in constant motion—colliding, overlapping, and competing. To track and influence them, one has to watch closely and acquire the skills to maneuver them in desired directions. Such maneuvering has become a time-consuming, intricate, and specialized practice. Yet learning the basic techniques is not difficult. Applying them successfully takes only common sense, practice, and time.

Effective participation in government decisionmaking has been made into a full-time job. Special interest groups, corporations, and even some universities are now represented by knowledgeable people whose primary responsibility is dealing with government. This chapter describes how any interested observers can become active participants in decisionmaking systems. It examines these systems at the national level, although the analysis is also applicable to most state and local governments.

## HOW TO LOCATE DECISIONMAKING SYSTEMS

Before one can participate in government decisionmaking, it is necessary to locate the system responsible for a particular policy and its related programs. The following steps should be helpful in the search:

107

1.  Define the issue as precisely as possible. Just what aspect of trade policy, for example, is the center of concern? Policies are implemented through legislated programs, which have been codified in law and added to the *U.S. Code.*

2.  Locate in the *U.S. Code* the law that established the program related to the policy in question.

3.  Look up the congressional subcommittees and the federal agencies responsible for overseeing, funding, and administering the program. If the program is administered through or by state government, find the state agency assigned responsibility for the program.

4.  Identify the corporations, trade associations, unions, nonprofit organizations, or other groups and individuals who are also interested in the program.

5.  Find out the names of program participants in Congress, the White House, state or federal regulatory agencies, and the interest group community. Learn something about them and the positions they take.

The *U.S. Code* is a compendium of legislation passed by Congress and signed by the president.[1] It can be used to find out which agency is responsible for managing the program. Another government publication, the *Congressional Quarterly Almanac*, contains useful information on other aspects of the decisionmaking system.[2] It identifies the subcommittee that heard the legislative proposals, and lists interest groups, executives, public officials, and others involved in the development of the legislation. The *Almanac* is a good chronicle of government decisionmaking systems.

Yet another helpful source is the *U.S. Government Manual.*[3] The *Manual* is the most comprehensive guide to the agencies, bureaus, and offices of government, including the Executive Office of the President. Included in the *Manual* are descriptions of the government agencies, some background on their histories, organizational charts, and a listing of top officials and their titles. The index to the *Manual* lists government agencies by subject area; for example, the heading, "Aviation," lists twelve agencies involved in that area. As a cross-reference, the section that describes agencies lists the programs for which each agency is responsible. All the agencies with any administrative responsibility for a specific program can be quickly located by using the *Manual.*

To become even more informed, read the congressional hearing and other committee reports. All these materials taken together will identify the programs, the participants, and the major concerns and responsibilities of each decisionmaking system.

Once the key agency is located, it is productive to call or visit the agency's public information office. The telephone number and name of the director of public information are listed in the *Manual.* This person can provide up-to-date information on the programs administered by the agency, including special features of the legislation, targeted groups, evaluation criteria, budget allocation, intergovernmental considerations, and important regulations.

Sometimes Congress is a more logical entry point into the decisionmaking system than the administrative agency. After locating the appropriate statute, one can identify from the *Congressional Directory* the committee or subcommittee that wrote the legislation and is responsible for oversight.[4] The members of the committee are also listed in the *Congressional Directory*, along with biographical information about each of them. The *Directory* is a very useful guide; it contains telephone numbers and office numbers of members of Congress by committee and by congressional district. The *Directory* is updated and published every session of Congress.

The *Congressional Staff Directory* is privately published and provides biographical information on the members of Congress and on the members of their office staffs and committee and subcommittee staffs.[5] Another informative publication about Capitol Hill is the *Almanac of American Politics*, which gives summaries of the members' voting records as well as their ratings by various constituency organizations like the Americans for Democratic Action and the Americans for Constitutional Action.[6] It is another source of biographical information on the members; in addition, it summarizes recent election results in each district and provides descriptions of each district.[7]

Once the appropriate entry point has been chosen, the next step is to make an appointment with a staff member on the Hill or a mid-level agency bureaucrat, either of whom can provide up-to-date information and, more importantly, the names and functions of all the other major participants in the decisionmaking system. Agency or congressional staff members are able to name the instrumental interest groups and how they are involved. Key White House people can also be identified. At this point, one must spend time gathering information about the decisionmaking system's past activities, future plans, and what seem to be the current issues on its agenda. This task is not as difficult as it might seem.

## TRACKING DECISIONMAKING SYSTEMS

One of the best sources for information on a decisionmaking system is the specialized press that has a vested interest in monitoring the particular system. Associated with nearly every decision system in Washington is a group of reporters from either trade publications or other independent publications for readers interested in a particular issue, such as aging or mass transit. The *Chronicle of Higher Education* and *Aviation News* are two prominent publications of this kind.

There are hundreds of these publications throughout the country. Talking with one of their reporters can yield important and timely information on either the purpose or progress of government programs as well as information on other issues that publication covers. Sometimes the best informed publication may be a relatively small newsletter operated out of a private home as a one-person business. The owner-reporter collects information by monitoring a decisionmaking system, writes it up, and turns copy over to a typing service. The typing service prepares camera-ready copy for the printer, who in turn delivers the finished newsletter to a mailing service. Though these operations are relatively small, they provide important specialized information that the larger media often cannot cover.

Two of the most important publications for those following or participating in decisionmaking systems are the *Congressional Quarterly* and the *National Journal*, both issued weekly by commercial publishers. They generally cover only the major and most controversial decision systems, but they also report on many actions and deliberations in Congress.

At this point one should have enough information to prepare a system diagram for a specific program by writing names, addresses, and telephone numbers of key participants beside the appropriate boxes. This diagram can be used as a map of the system in question (see Figure 8-1). Now the time has come to follow the system care-

**Figure 8-1.** A Government Decisionmaking System.

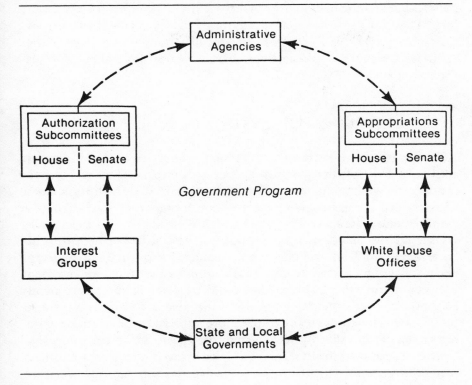

fully and to meet regularly with its participants. Learn what is on their minds: how they see the future of the program; how they would like to see it changed; and how they plan to move ahead in the coming months. These discussions will help one assess the influence of these various individuals and begin to build the kind of analytical and forecasting capabilities that others participating in these systems have developed over time.

There are also consulting and lobbying firms that track decision-making systems for clients. Larger organizations do their own tracking, but these firms can be helpful to smaller corporations not interested in setting up a Washington office. They prepare reports for their clients on specific issues by compiling information from the regular media, the specialized media, government reports, the *Congressional Record*, the *Federal Register*, and other sources. If a client wants to become more actively involved, these organizations will set up appointments, arrange for the client's appearance at agency or congressional hearings, and even help write testimony for the hearings. The major representational groups, like the U.S. Chamber of Commerce, the National Association of Manufacturers, and the AFL-CIO, also track and participate in these decisionmaking systems for their members.

## DECISIONMAKING SYSTEMS IN ACTION

After locating the system and learning about its background and agenda, it is helpful to gain some additional information on the environment in which the system operates. The U.S. Constitution does not establish or even encourage the development of a coordinated management system. In fact, the structure of divided or shared powers set up by the Constitution makes it very difficult at times for government officials to effectively manage programs. An ongoing debate in political science and public administration circles has been between those who want to invest more power in the positions of top officials—presidents, governors, and mayors—to enable them to manage government programs more effectively, and those who prefer the decentralized power system the Constitution encourages.

The decisionmaking systems that have evolved over the years form a middle ground; they informally bridge the separated powers required by the Constitution. It is through these systems that the separated institutions of government come together to make compromises, develop public policy, and manage programs. Decisionmaking systems thus make government more stable and predictable.

The systems operate in a constitutionally created environment of uncertainty and flux that constantly threatens to destabilize them or at least reduce their effectiveness. They are mainly held together by government officials who fear what would happen to the programs they are responsible for if the systems disintegrated. These officials know that such a disintegration would also destroy the stability necessary for effective government management. Cooperation and compromise would be all but impossible; the participants would lose control of their programs, and decisions of the system would become much less predictable. There are those who benefit from chaos in government—benefiting from delays in program implementation, for example—but they are not usually the key decision-makers in the system.

Insiders place a high premium on keeping the decisionmaking structure together. Whenever a new proposal surfaces, their first thoughts are: "How much do I disagree with this proposal? Do I disagree with it strongly enough to interrupt the effective operation of the decisionmaking system? Or can I bend and compromise with others to keep the decisionmaking structure functioning smoothly?" If disagreement among the participants becomes too intense, the system can lose its control over the programs for which it is responsible. Consequently, there are substantial built-in incentives for compromise.

The government officials charged with program responsibilities are not alone in wanting to keep the decision systems as stable as possible. It is considerably easier for outsiders from the private sector to deal with the smaller decision systems than with the larger, less organized institutions of government. Consequently, these outsiders are often strong allies so long as they like the results of the system's activities.

For instance, consider the private companies that do contract work for NASA. They only have to deal with a few key members of Congress, some of the congressional staff, NASA executives, and other longtime participants in the NASA decision system. What if that system were to collapse? Space program activities would become solely the responsibility of Congress and the executive branch: in other words, the responsibility of almost everyone in government and consequently of no one. The NASA contractors would be compelled to work with ill-defined and shifting coalitions among the 535 members of Congress plus staff. It would be extraordinarily difficult to know who was in charge of what. Stability and predictability would be lost.

So one of the first concerns of a corporation that is successfully participating in the government space program is to support and maintain the NASA decision system, which includes the corresponding congressional committees and White House staff. The *Challenger* shuttle disaster in January 1986 could lead to major changes in the space program and its decisionmaking system. NASA contractors are closely watching the policy and organizational changes that have already occurred.

When cyanide-contaminated Tylenol capsules caused the 1983 deaths of seven people in the Chicago area, the decision system—which revolved around the Food and Drug Administration and also included Tylenol's manufacturer, Johnson and Johnson— suffered a severe shock. The system that had successfully maintained drug purity over the years was immediately called into question and seemed to lose control—but only temporarily, as it turned out.

When the disaster first struck, Johnson and Johnson executives called on about 250 members of Congress, nearly all the governors and their state health officials, and local health officials in several major cities. They needed to assure all concerned that new packaging laws and regulations were not necessary. Arguing that the FDA-based system could handle the crisis with the industry's cooperation, they restored both public and government confidence in the small decision system that had successfully managed pure drug programs for decades. Responsibility for an issue that seemed to have exploded far beyond the control of the system was returned to that system by the conscientious efforts of the manufacturers and the government. No new regulations were adopted. When more cyanide-laced Tylenol capsules were discovered in early 1986, Johnson and Johnson moved quickly to forestall a rerun of the 1983 crisis by announcing that it would no longer market the product in capsule form.

Presidents also sometimes benefit by having a decision system to work with instead of being forced to deal with the larger government institutions. Early in his term, President Carter became frustrated with the niggling regulations of the Occupational Safety and Health Administration. The rules requiring portable toilets on the range for cowhands, and certain stepladder strength-versus-angle specifications, were widely criticized and derided as silly consequences of government regulation. Carter eventually issued an executive order that eliminated about 40 percent of OSHA's rules. Before doing so, he had negotiated the terms of the executive order with those in the decision system, thereby devising a more sensible program for OSHA. The key decisionmakers, already accustomed to working with each other, were also willing to work with the president at his request.

Having decisionmaking systems makes it possible to locate responsibility for programs within the relatively small group of individuals involved. This feature of decisionmaking systems benefits corporations, the president, and even the general public. When it is possible to know who is in charge of a government program, and how to reach that person, government can more easily be kept accountable to the public. Transferring responsibility for programs to the larger institutions of government could lead to program neglect and the weakening of government management structures. Nearly everyone, including the public, loses in those circumstances.

## INITIATING CHANGE IN THE DECISIONMAKING SYSTEMS

But there is another side to the story. Decision systems that close out new participants and become impervious to change may be denying their accountability; poor management can result from such intransigence. When this happens, changing a decision system is easier than one might think. The Constitution encourages stability in the workings of government, but it also provides opportunities for necessary changes. There are essentially two methods for bringing about change in decision systems and their outcomes.

One approach is to work with the system: supporting it while working toward incremental change from within. There are several ways of doing this, some of the more obvious being to work for the reelection of the elected members of the system, provide information to strengthen the system, or persuade others to support the system by building broader coalitions. There are many access points through which individuals or groups can voice their wishes for change. They can testify before administrative and congressional committee hearings, or they can call on executive, congressional, or agency staff to try to persuade them to modify their positions.

When working within the decisionmaking system fails to achieve results, the other approach is to find or create an alternative decisionmaking structure. If the original system loses the chance to process the issue, the outcome is likely to be radically different. The first approach is more prudent and most often selected. The second is chosen only at considerable risk and bears a much greater chance of losing the fight.

In 1967 President Lyndon B. Johnson was faced with such a choice. His advisors had developed a proposal for granting the District of Columbia a modicum of home rule that involved changing the commission form of government to a mayor-council form, with the top officials appointed by the president. Past efforts to reorganize the District of Columbia government had been thwarted by recalcitrant members of the House District Committee, parliamentary maneuvers, the Washington Board of Trade, and grass roots lobbying. Any further attempt at change would require a strategy different from the legislative route through the District committees of Congress.

Johnson's advisors understood decisionmaking systems and knew that the odds were against being able to navigate a D.C. governmental reform bill through the established system. The only legitimate alternative was processing the issue through another system. They recommended that the president introduce a reorganization plan for D.C. government to Congress by way of the House Committee on Government Operations, where it would probably receive a much more favorable hearing than it would if sent to the House District Committee. The strategy worked. By finding an alternative decisionmaking system, the president and his advisors achieved their goal of finally reorganizing the ninety-three-year-old governmental system in the District of Columbia.[8]

### Redefining the Issue

When decisionmaking systems fail to respond to attempts at incremental change, more extreme strategies are required. One such strategy is redefining the issue. All public issues can be defined in at least two, and usually several, ways. For instance, the debate over requiring health warnings on cigarette packages and in advertising was for many years defined solely as a commercial issue. The focus was on the commercial aspects of cigarettes: growing tobacco leaf, manufacturing the cigarettes, advertising, and then selling them.[9]

Regulation of cigarette packaging and advertising can also, however, be defined as a health issue. Since for some time now there has been little doubt among medical researchers and practitioners that smoking is harmful to health, there have been frequent attempts to require health warnings on cigarette packages. For many years these proposals were put before a decisionmaking system that handled commercial and economic issues. The decision from that system was predictable: nothing changed. This was a logical decision from a system more attuned to the health of the economy than to personal health. Once the issue was redefined as a health issue, however, things began to change. A new decision system with a different outlook assumed control of the issue. Eventually, the warnings and other health-related goals were attained.

Redefining the issue can transfer it to a different decisionmaking system whose participants may be more likely to respond positively to refocused information and different viewpoints. Another example is the food stamp program, which was formed to distribute surplus food to the poor and the needy. The program was delegated to the Department of Agriculture to administer. In the 1960s Americans became much more aware of the scope and intensity of poverty across the country. Many liberal interest groups saw the food stamp program as an obvious vehicle for relieving hunger and ameliorating poverty. These groups felt that the Agriculture Department was too conservative in its approach to surplus food distribution. Representative Jamie L. Whitten (D–Miss.), chairman of the House Appropriations Subcommittee on Agriculture at the time and often called the "permanent secretary of agriculture," strongly supported the Agriculture Department's point of view.

The battle was joined. The liberals saw the food stamp program as part of a social welfare policy that should be administered by the Department of Health, Education, and Welfare. The conservatives viewed it as a surplus food program to be handled by the Agriculture Department. For more than a decade the issue was the subject of intense debate, hyperbole, compromise, and vote trading, with minor adjustments occasionally being made to satisfy pressures from competing clientele groups. The liberal groups have not been successful in redefining the food stamp program so that it can become part of a social welfare decisionmaking system.[10] They have achieved one modest victory, however: since 1979 very low-income recipients no longer have to pay for their food stamps.

### Reorganizing

Another strategy for changing decisionmaking systems is to build new coalitions with other interested parties and then work to move a program from one decisionmaking system to another or to create an entirely new system. Government's reorganization of itself often has this purpose. Moving a program from one bureau to another or from one subcommittee to another results in a change of participants, coalitions, and probably the outcomes. A federal program to relieve traffic congestion in large cities, for example, would substantially change in emphasis if it were moved from a highway-oriented decisionmaking system to one concerned with mass transit. It is easy to see how officials from the Urban Mass Transportation Administration, the U.S. Conference of Mayors, and the American Public Transit Association, with the support of sympathetic legislators, might propose solutions very different from those offered by the Federal Highway Administration, state highway departments, the American Automobile Association, and their congressional allies.

In 1978, when the Carter administration proposed the creation of a separate Department of Education, many supported the bill in the hope that it would give education issues greater visibility and more political clout. Others supported the bill because they felt it would spotlight numerous educational programs that were not receiving the rigorous evaluations they might deserve.

This reorganization proposal was opposed by a number of special interest groups and by the Departments of Defense and Agriculture, whose educational programs were scheduled to be transferred to the new Department of Education. Sensing that their decisionmaking systems might be reorganized out of existence, these groups fought to preserve their turf, existing power relationships, and institutionalized channels of access. Others opposed the new department out of the fear that it would create another large bureaucracy. The proposal was not enacted in the rush to adjourn the Ninety-fifth Congress, despite great pressure to do so from the Carter administration and the National Education Association. The pros and cons had been articulated, however, and the political struggle continued in the next session of Congress, culminating in the creation of the Department of Education in 1979.[11]

The importance of reorganization or redirection as a strategy for change cannot be overemphasized. Greater efficiency, or adherence to some allegedly scientific principles of administration, are the most common arguments for shifting an activity from one bureau to another or for creating a new governmental unit. In reality, government organization reflects national priorities and problems. The creation of the Department of Energy was a confirmation that energy policy had become sufficiently important to warrant its own cabinet-level agency, instead of being treated piecemeal by several agencies concerned primarily with other matters. Other issues elevated to cabinet status within the past twenty years include housing and urban development and transportation, while environmental protection, occupational safety, and equal employment opportunity are some of the issues now receiving their own lower-level but separate agencies.

### Escalating the Controversy

A third strategy is to escalate the controversy over an unresolved issue to a higher level of decisionmaking. The president, secretaries of cabinet departments, and congressional leaders are not directly involved in decisionmaking systems. Their role in trying to bring about change is similar, operationally, to that of outsiders trying to influence the systems. They use the strategies of persuasion, redefinition, reorganization, and coalition-building that others employ. One major difference, however, is that these individuals, because of their high-level positions in government, are much more powerful than the ordinary participant. Those interested in bringing about major change usually attempt to get these powerful government leaders involved on behalf of their position, to change the focus of the issue, the balance of power and influence, and hence the outcome.

Two striking examples of this strategy in operation are the War on Poverty and the Medicare programs. In both cases the decisionmaking systems began to process these issues as they would any major piece of domestic legislation. One important difference between each of these and hundreds of other proposals was that billions of dollars were involved; each program was to be financed by redistributing money from people paying higher taxes to people in need who paid relatively low taxes.[12] When the political stakes are high and a major redistribution of tax dollars is involved, it is difficult for the lower-level decisionmaking systems to generate the compromises and consensus necessary to produce a bill. When deadlock occurs on such issues of national importance, it usually means that the decisionmaking must be elevated to a higher level. Congressional leadership, the cabinet, and probably the president become involved. At this higher level, any compromise reached is likely to be very broad in scope.

The Economic Opportunity Act of 1964, the centerpiece of the War on Poverty, exemplifies such a situation. The appropriate decisionmaking system could resolve many small conflicts but was unable to bridge the wide ideological chasm between conservative and liberal members of Congress. As Ripley and Franklin point out:

> Individual members of the House and Senate, particularly those in strategic committee positions, were important in helping make decisions, as were individuals scattered throughout the administration and relevant executive-branch agencies. However, these individuals could not make binding decisions by themselves: a much broader set of decision makers got involved, including all senators and representatives (through floor action), the president and his top advisors, and a large variety of interest groups.[13]

An analysis of the passage of the Medicare program reveals the operation of the same kind of forces that brought about War on Poverty legislation. Once again a piece of social welfare legislation, involving billions of dollars, was stalemated this time in a conflict over the scope of a federally supported health insurance program. The AFL–CIO, the National Council of Senior Citizens, and a host of public welfare organizations were in favor of such a program. Opposing any federal adoption of a national insurance program were the American Medical Association, the insurance industry, and most of the business community.[14]

Two factors helped to resolve the conflict. First, this issue had been debated in Congress and the White House intermittently since 1935. Very few new ideas and arguments were being raised for or against the issue. Second, in 1964 the American people elected an overwhelmingly Democratic majority in both houses of Congress. This new majority had a liberal outlook and a determination to enact social legislation, and it was ready to work with a president sympathetic to Medicare.

Recognizing that the tide was going against them, opponents sought the best possible compromise. They did so by removing the issue from decisionmaking systems that specialized in health issues and elevating it to the highest levels of governmental decisionmaking. The strategy proved successful: the final Medicare bill contained more amendments acceptable to its opponents than it otherwise would have.

Decisionmaking systems routinely process most of the government's programs. Those involved invest much time and effort in supporting the systems that produce benefits and also in attempting to change those that do not. Corporate lobbyists focus most of their activities on the decision systems and are largely satisfied with the output or decisions of those systems. There are, however, a growing number of issues that for many reasons are not processed well or at all by the established decision systems of government. These more complicated problems and programs fall to the larger institutions of government for resolution— with very uneven results.

## NOTES

1.  *U.S. Code of Federal Regulations* (Washington, D.C.: Office of the Federal Register, National Archives and Records Service, General Services Administration).
2.  *Congressional Quarterly Almanac* (Washington, D.C.: Congressional Quarterly, Inc., published annually).
3.  Office of the Federal Register, National Archives and Records Service, General Services Administration, *U.S. Government Manual* (Washington, D.C.: U.S. Government Printing Office, published annually).
4.  United States Congress, *Official Congressional Directory* (Washington, D.C.: U.S. Government Printing Office, published annually).
5.  Charles B. Brownson, ed., *Congressional Staff Directory* (Mount Vernon, Va.: Congressional Staff Directory, published annually).
6.  Michael Barone and Grant Ujifusa, *The Almanac of American Politics* (Washington, D.C.: National Journal, published annually).
7.  A good guide to all of these information sources is *Federal Focus: A Guide to Government Information and Activity* (Washington, D.C.: U.S. Chamber of Commerce, 1985).
8.  For a discussion of this strategy, see Royce Hanson and Bernard H. Ross, "Washington," in Donald C. Rowat, ed., *The Government of Federal Capitals* (Toronto, Canada: University of Toronto Press, 1973), pp. 93–99.
9.  Fritschler, *Smoking and Politics: Policymaking and the Federal Bureaucracy*, 3d ed. (Englewood Cliffs, N.J.: Prentice-Hall, 1983), pp. 37–41.
10. For an excellent discussion of this issue, see Nick Kotz, *Let Them Eat Promises: The Politics of Hunger in America* (New York: Anchor Books, 1971); see also Phillip M. Gregg, "What Difference Will Food Stamp Reform Make?" *The Bureaucrat* 7 (Winter 1978): 22–33.
11. For a discussion of the arguments surrounding the proposal for a new Department of Education, see Joel Havemann, "Carter's Reorganization Plans—Scrambling for Turf," *National Journal* 10 (1978): 788–92.
12. For a discussion of redistributive domestic policy, see Randall B. Ripley and Grace A. Franklin, *Congress, the Bureaucracy, and Public Policy*, 3d ed. (Homewood, Ill.: Dorsey Press, 1984), pp. 170–182.

13.   Ripley and Franklin, p. 172. For a discussion of the War on Poverty legislation, see Sar A. Levitan, *The Great Society's Poor Law* (Baltimore: Johns Hopkins University Press, 1968), and Daniel P. Moynihan, *Maximum Feasible Misunderstanding: Community Action in the War on Poverty* (New York: The Free Press, 1969), ch. 5.

14.   For a discussion of the Medicare struggle, see Ted Marmor, *The Politics of Medicare*, rev. ed. (Chicago: Aldine, 1973); see also Eric Redman, *The Dance of Legislation* (New York: Simon and Schuster, 1973).

# 9 STRENGTHS AND WEAKNESSES
A Critique of Government
Decisionmaking Systems

The decisionmaking systems examined in this book have played a large role in our country's development. They both incorporate and reflect the special mixture of ideology and pragmatism that characterizes American political life. As they provide avenues for democratic participation and popular control, they also compete with each other and share decisionmaking powers, guaranteeing that no one group or individual can control the government. The systems preserve the ideals of those who wrote the Constitution: they disperse, fragment, and regulate power. At the same time the decisionmaking systems provide government with a management structure for program administration that is relatively efficient and adaptable to the demands of our complex modern era.

The decisionmaking systems work remarkably well at reconciling the conflicting goals of democratically dispersed power on the one hand, and management efficiency on the other. In spite of their shortcomings, decision systems are reasonably successful at implementing well-defined programs in established areas such as health, agriculture, education, and road building. In addition to specific definitions and scope, such programs also have widely understood purposes and a reliable set of clientele or supporters.

Given the problems of governing a complex, multi-interest, and diversified society, the small decisionmaking systems that have evolved over the years are impressive in their management of this kind of program, which, fortunately, represents most government activity. The internal and interactive operations of the existing decision systems sustain the basic tenets of democratic government.

## PLURALISM, BARGAINING, AND INCREMENTALISM

The program-focused decision systems are pluralistic, depend upon bargaining strategies, and move incrementally. They provide access for a pluralistic variety of economic, social, and ethnic groups, each trying to advance its own interests. These groups must bargain with each other over their conflicting interests, through their legislative and bureaucratic allies, whether to gain as many of their objectives as possible or to protect their interests. Such groups are by no means evenly matched, but rarely is one so dominant as to gain more than gradual incremental change in an established policy area.

Pluralism and bargaining are both necessary to the health of a democratic society. One of the most articulate observers of our government processes is political economist Charles Lindblom, who described this system of bargaining as one guided by "the science of muddling through."[1] This approach, he says, is preferable to the more rational, comprehensive planning strategies frequently suggested as alternative methods of setting policy. For one thing, "muddling through" guarantees a certain amount of stability in a given policy area because change remains a slow and difficult process. This incremental approach guards against sudden, radical changes in the government's way of addressing problems, thus democratically ensuring that all interested groups have the opportunity to participate in policymaking. Government decisions evolve out of compromises reached by all interested groups and individuals instead of being made by a few technicians who are not accountable to the public. Perhaps the most important point of Lindblom's argument is that rational comprehensive planning simply will not work for the U.S. government:

> It is impossible to take everything important into consideration unless "important" is so narrowly defined that analysis is in fact quite limited. Limits on human intellectual capacities and on available information set definite limits to man's capacity to be comprehensive.[2]

Bargaining and incrementalism quite naturally tend to maintain the status quo. This stability is sometimes called "stagnation," for agencies and programs established in response to yesterday's problems often prove incapable of changing to meet today's crises. Public agencies must operate in a turbulent social, political, and technological environment. To justify their high administrative costs, some say that agencies should be able to forecast and adapt to this turbulence.

Pluralism and bargaining can also seem like wasted efforts when government decisions prove to be contradictory. One policymaking decision system succeeds in establishing a program—ostensibly in the public interest—that might diminish the effectiveness of another program that was also initiated in the public interest. For example, the effectiveness of money spent on cancer research and on antismoking campaigns is partially negated by the government's program of tobacco price supports and marketing assistance. To carry this example a step further, the elimination or reduction of tobacco price supports would undercut economic development efforts and exacerbate unemployment in the tobacco-growing and tobacco-processing regions.

Legitimate interests are represented in both the health and economic aspects of the issue, but thus far the government has not come up with any long-range solutions. Establishing programs through which tobacco farmers and tobacco industry workers could switch to producing other products, without suffering undue economic hardships, would be one such solution. But the economic interests continue to win their price supports, and the health interests continue to receive funding and support for their education programs. This dichotomy is mostly attributable to the difficulty of coordinating policies that are processed by different decisionmaking systems.

Some question the ability of reformers to bring about fundamental or major changes in decisionmaking, given the static nature of the systems. Programs do tend to take on a life of their own, which makes it difficult, although not impossible, to eliminate them. In an effort to determine whether government organizations are immortal, Herbert Kaufman, a noted political scientist, studied the major subdivisions of ten executive departments in the federal government. (Only the Defense Department was excluded.) He found that of the 175 subdivisions existing in 1923, there were 148—almost 85 percent—still operating in 1973. Furthermore, most of the activities of the twenty-seven terminated departments were not abandoned; they were reassigned to other units.[3] Once government becomes involved in a policy area as a regulator, a provider of services, or a subsidizer, the chances are very good that it will stay involved.

Part of this organizational longevity is attributable to the bureaucrats' desire for job security and what some perceive as their propensity for empire building. But government employees acting alone cannot keep an unpopular or unproductive program afloat, much less expand it. They need allies, both on Capitol Hill and among organized private interests. Opinion differs widely, of course, on which programs are unpopular or unproductive. A dairy farmer might decide that too much money is spent on aid to families with dependent children and not enough is spent on milk price supports, while a welfare recipient would very likely reach the opposite conclusion. As a general rule, however, the proponents of a given government program feel more strongly about it than do its opponents. The typical government program provides substantial benefits to a relatively small group while imposing only small incremental burdens, such as higher taxes or higher prices, on the vast majority. Sometimes these increments do add up and produce political backlashes, which usually threaten the most politically vulnerable programs instead of the most deserving or costly ones. For the most part though, the U.S. governmental system tends to perpetuate programs rather than terminate them.

As noted earlier, decisionmaking systems do not perform well when a policy requires the coordination of programs run by more than three or four established systems. To control inflation or lower the federal deficit, for example, the government needs to synchronize large numbers of separate programs. Trade-offs must be made between programs. There are structures and procedures for accomplishing this kind of objective, but they tend to be weak and ill defined. The president and congressional leader must bring many disparate programs together to accomplish the overarching goals of policy. The U.S. government is not well equipped to deal routinely with large, complex problems because, as a rule, they require a high degree of coordination and centralized leadership. The U.S. system intentionally makes the resolution of such problems difficult.

One of the surest ways to stem the growth of existing programs and inhibit the creation of new ones is to convince Congress and the public that the country cannot afford them. President Reagan has accomplished his agenda of cutting back governmental domestic activities by letting the national debt grow and then pointing to it as a reason to stem program growth and development. Supply-side economic practices, the tax cut of 1981, and substantial increases in defense spending all combined to produce a doubling of the national debt in the first Reagan term. The debt continues to grow at the rate of between $150 and $200 billion each year. The size and persistence of the debt has made it politically feasible for Congress and President Reagan to cut popular domestic programs in spite of opposition that had previously been able to block such cuts. Disciplining decision systems and using them as vehicles for a president's views is a clumsy and dramatic political tactic. Furthermore, this tactic is unlikely to succeed very often; but it has succeeded rather well for President Reagan.[4]

In the government's administration of routine programs, decisionmaking characterized by pluralism, bargaining, and incrementalism serves the country well. The decisionmaking systems process most issues in a fair and efficient manner, notwithstanding the possibility that from time to time a major corrective action—like that initiated by the Reagan administration—is a useful thing.

## GOVERNMENT'S RESPONSE TO BIG ISSUES

There are, however, large areas of government decisionmaking where decision systems do not work well, if at all. Major issues concerning war and delicate diplomatic maneuvers must be orchestrated by the president and his closest associates. The president can accomplish what the formal decisionmaking system cannot in these areas. He can get key people involved quickly and then synthesize their ideas and opinions in much less time than if the issue had to be processed by other decision systems.

When domestic issues grow too large and become publicly controversial, the decisionmaking systems are inadequate. Trying to satisfy too many conflicting interests can grind any government system to a halt. When the political stakes are high, decision processes fail to coordinate, plan, and manage. They themselves prove to be too large, unwieldy, and conflict ridden for handling the demands made on them by these issues.

Energy policy is an issue that affects almost all government actions. In addition to its domestic and international ramifications, energy policy creates important consequences for both the national economy and the economic well-being of individuals. Energy is simply too big for one or even several related decisionmaking systems to handle. Similarly, trade policy is difficult to develop because it involves so many competing programs and decision systems.

Tax reform is another difficult goal, given the existing decision systems. Historically, tax matters have been handled by the type of small systems described in the preceding chapters. Changes in tax policy were incremental; small adjustments or additions were made in the margins of the tax code. The major tax reform proposed by President Reagan in 1985 could not be handled in the traditional way because the proposed changes wee too substantial and far reaching. Consequently, tax reform discussions were held by the appropriate House and Senate committees, with the active participation of the congressional leadership, top administration officials, and a large House/Senate conference committee. Eventually, extensive debate also took place on the floor of both houses of Congress.

When large issues like energy, tax reform, or trade policy become politically active, the decision systems must give responsibility over to large, less systematic decision processes that include many more people as well as the highest echelons of government. The president, leaders of Congress, and cabinet secretaries become directly involved in policymaking instead of leaving it all up to the bureau chiefs and other officials at lower levels. Debate occurs on the floor of the House and the Senate at earlier stages in the policymaking processes; normally, only pro forma floor action is taken after committees and subcommittees have done their work. A large number of interest groups also become actively involved when an issue is important. All this extra activity is often time consuming, chaotic, and unpredictable in its outcome.

Big issues lack identifiable political or social boundaries. They do not respond to piecemeal solutions as do many smaller social and political issues; neither are past solutions helpful in solving modern problems. There is a major difference between issues, like energy, trade, and troubled cities of the Northeast, on the one hand, and the Great Depression of the 1920s and 1930s on the other.

The federal government's operational response to the depression was very conventional. Several new programs were created during that period to solve various discrete problems created by the depression. The social security program was established, along with guaranteed bank deposit programs, the Works Progress Administration, the Civilian Conservation Corps, the Securities and Exchange Commission, and other programs designed to bring the nation out of the great economic collapse. There were few attempts to coordinate these programs, since a program-by-program solution was sufficient. They operated independently of each other, within the conventional decisionmaking systems. Franklin D. Roosevelt did little to change government decisionmaking processes or their operations. He created more systems, and consequently there was more government at the end of the Great Depression than there was before it started. But this change was simply more of the same. Energy policy development in the 1970s is a remarkably different story.

President Carter's effort to develop a national energy policy revealed the inability of decisionmaking systems to process a large issue that is difficult to break up into smaller, discrete, manageable areas. The importance of cheap energy to the American economy and life-style is overwhelming. Energy supply affects the way we live, what we eat, how we dress, our transportation system, U.S. international relations—the list goes on and on. No government decisionmaking system is large enough to encompass all or even a major portion of the issues directly tied to energy. Consequently, the government seemed to be floundering when President Carter pressed for the development of an energy policy; it could not come up with a coherent policy. Some programs, such as highway building and natural gas price regulation, promoted energy consumption while other programs—tax write-offs for home insulation, for example, and a host of publicity campaigns—favored conservation.

Senator William Proxmire, appearing on "Face the Nation" in July 1978, was asked why Congress had failed to pass the president's energy program. Proxmire's reply demonstrates what happens when too many issues are grouped together into a "national policy" and a decision system is asked to process the policy as a whole:

> Three parts of that program can be passed right away. I wrote to the president, together with other senators, urging that he separate that program into its parts. We can pass energy conservation, coal conversion; and we can pass the utility rate reform. What we can't pass is the deregulation of natural gas and the crude oil equalization tax. And if the president insists on that, we won't pass an energy bill at all this year. If he separates it out we'll pass something.[5]

Proxmire was telling the reporters that energy policy was too large and conflict ridden to fit into the decisionmaking system. If broken down into more discrete and identifiable programs, these issues could have been more easily processed by the appropriate decisionmaking systems.

The politics behind the creation of the Department of Energy illustrate the problem clearly. In the spring of 1977 the proposal was debated on the Hill and attacked in a very conventional manner. The congressional criticism of the Carter proposal was that the Department of Energy would be too powerful; the new Secretary of Energy would have more power than is traditional or desirable in the American scheme of things.

Senator John Glenn, a member of the committee that wrote the bill, maintained that Congress would not be creating an energy czar. He argued that, in fact, the proposed Department of Energy would be weak because it would not have enough legislated power to deal with some of the major aspects of energy policy. As an example, he pointed out that 40 percent of the nation's crude oil, after refinement, is consumed by automobiles. The Department of Transportation, not the Energy Department, would continue to police standards for automobile fuel efficiency. Omitting this responsibility from the Energy Department's jurisdiction immediately removed a major component of energy policy from the new agency's control. By the same token, offshore oil leases would still be under the control of the Department of the Interior. There was considerable debate over who should set the wellhead price of natural gas — the Federal Power Commission or the newly created Department of Energy. A compromise was reached on that point, with a semi-independent commission created within the new department to handle the task.

Congressional response to the creation of the Department of Energy was typical: no national energy policy was developed. Government has also failed to produce a national health, urban, or transportation policy. Historically, we have preferred to divide power and deal with issues at a low level in the decisionmaking process. Energy is probably one of those issues that cannot be handled well that way, yet the creation of a cabinet-level department that controls all aspects of energy policy has proven to be unthinkable in contemporary political terms.

Trade is another policy problem with no good programmatic solutons. In only three and one-half years, from 1981 to mid-1985, the

United States went from being the world's largest net creditor nation to becoming a net debtor nation. The deterioration in the U.S. international trade position resulted from several factors at home and abroad, certainly including the high value of the dollar during that period.

Several proposals were made to deal with the trade problem, including a proposal to transform the Department of Commerce into a Department of Trade. This idea was put before President Reagan with arguments from his staff similar to those heard earlier from the Carter advisors on energy. Reagan decided to not go ahead with the plan. His reluctance probably was based in part on the knowledge that trade is too diffuse an issue to be dealt with by reorganizing trade programs into one cabinet department.

The decision systems that can process tobacco price supports or a cancer research program are just not suited to an issue as far reaching as trade. Figure 9-1 depicts the futility of constructing a decision system diagram for trade along the lines of the model put forth in Figure 6-1. It does not work because there are too many departments and agencies, congressional committees, advisory groups, and special interests involved. In this hypothetical decision system, trade policy would be administered in a contradictory and piecemeal fashion, with controversies occasionally reaching the floor of Congress and the Oval Office. Results would be incremental, duplicative, and frustrating. No government—and especially not the decentralized government of the United States—would be able to handle an issue like trade as smoothly as it handles smaller, more specific issues.

Similar to energy and trade policy in its implications for government decisionmaking systems is the issue of deterioration in the northeastern and north central cities. Most of these cities are small geographically and surrounded by large suburban jurisdictions with governments of their own. Over the years various federal and state policies have inadvertently encouraged both the middle class and industry to leave the central cities and relocate in the suburbs. This is, of course, a serious problem for these cities; the tax base deteriorates while public service expenses are likely to increase.

The GI Bill of Rights passed after World War II was designed to reward veterans and reassimilate them into American life. But this legislation, like some other government programs, had unintended and serious consequences for geographically small cities—those that could not expand their boundaries to keep fleeing residents in their

**Figure 9-1.** U.S. Foreign Trade Decisionmaking.

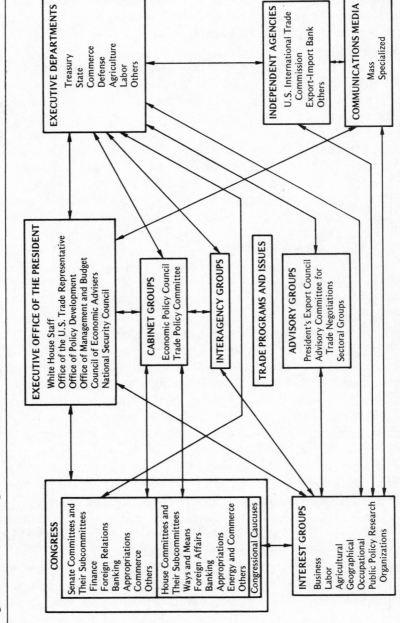

tax base. The no-down-payment home mortgage provision of the GI Bill put the federal government in the business of encouraging the middle class to leave the cities for larger, more attractive suburban housing. One could read accounts of congressional debates on the GI Bill and not find the word *cities* mentioned anywhere. Why not? The GI Bill was considered by a veterans' decisionmaking system that did its job well but had no interest or expertise in the problems of central cities. Highway programs and urban mass transit programs make it easier for the middle class to move in and out of cities and for industry to locate itself in suburban areas. Such programs have been discussed and decided by their respective decisionmaking systems: again, with little concern for their impact on the central cities. Even today there is no one department of the national government devoted to urban problems and issues.

Government regulation of business has the same kind of problem. Individual agency regulations, although sometimes unpopular, are not overly troublesome to industry as a whole. There are complaints about specific programs and the way they are run, but these complaints usually involve only questions of incremental change, fine-tuning, and amendment. What is proving to be one of the most serious problems with business regulation is competition and contradiction among regulations. Closely related is the government's inability to see the cumulative effects of regulations on particular corporations. There is an analogy in medicine. Every legally dispensed drug sold in the United States is tested by the government before it is declared safe. Consumers can know reasonably well what will happen when they take a certain drug. But what happens when someone takes a combination of different drugs in the same day? Very often no one really knows what the result might be.

These kinds of large, complex, and interconnected problems challenge not only the efficacy but even the continued existence of the decentralized government structure, which operates through small, competing decision systems. More often than not, steps taken to improve government decisionmaking systems involve placing more power in the hands of fewer people. These steps may improve the effectiveness of government programs, but they lead us away from the tradition of regulating government power by distributing it among several competing systems.

## IMPROVING GOVERNMENT DECISIONMAKING

There are different ways to streamline and reform government to make it more responsive to the major problems and issues facing the nation. One way is to apply better management techniques to the existing structures: improving the way programs are managed and introducing techniques for better coordinating the work of diverse and competing decisionmaking systems. Management improvement techniques employed by government are often borrowed from business; others are unique to the public sector. Most of these techniques do not change the basic structure of decision systems.

Another approach is to create new institutions oversee and coordinate the existing systems, and even transfer some decisionmaking authority over to the new centralized entity. In the recent past the decisionmaking authority of the president has been strengthened by investing the office with additional powers or by adding staff units. Congress has undertaken similar reforms. The size of congressional staff has increased substantially, and the formal oversight institutions of Congress, like the General Accounting Office, have been given more power. Furthermore, Congress centralized its budget processes in 1975 and created a new support agency called the Congressional Budget Office. These reforms have reduced the importance and impact of the specialized decisionmaking systems, permitting the president and congressional leaders to exercise greater authority.

Management improvement in the federal government has a long history that parallels the history of management improvement in the private sector. Government pioneered the program-oriented budget system called Planning Program Budgeting Systems (PPBS) and adopted the Zero-Based Budgeting (ZBB) system developed by private industry. Government has also tried to implement cost-benefit analysis and management by objectives.

One of the most publicized government attempts at management improvement was the work of the Grace Commission, also known as the President's Private Sector Survey on Cost Control. The commission enlisted the volunteer efforts of 161 top executives and other experts from the private sector. Thirty-six task forces issued a forty-seven-volume report covering management practices in all the major agencies of government. The 1984 summary report stated that implementing the commission's recommendations would result in net savings—savings plus revenue increases—of more than $424 billion in three years.[6]

The recommendations of the commission were not as valuable as they could have been because the final report confused policy changes with management improvement. For example, the largest part of the proposed $424 billion savings was in the recommendation to close "unnecessary" military bases in the United States. What is or is not a necessary military base is a policy debate that has raged in and out of Congress for decades; it surely is much more than a management improvement issue.

Two congressional agencies, the General Accounting Office and the Congressional Budget Office, analyzed the Grace Commission recommendations and concluded that about two-thirds of them had some merit. Some had been recommended before by others, who had also discovered that most of the potential savings would require changes in law and policies enacted by Congress. The Grace Commission was less effective than it might have been because it focused more on what government does than on how it does it.[7]

Less visible but probably more effective than the Grace Commission survey are the efforts of the Office of Management and Budget. Ever since OMB was created out of the old Bureau of the Budget during the Nixon administration, this White House agency has devoted much attention to management improvement throughout government. A recent OMB report on management discusses several past accomplishments as well as future goals for government managers.[8] In addition to the President's "Management Message," the report lists the accomplishments and plans of two presidential councils—one on Integrity and Efficiency and another on Management Improvement. It also includes a report on the President's Productivity Improvement Program and a summary of the status of management reviews currently under way in twenty-three major federal agencies. In 1985 accomplishments of the presidential councils ranged from putting $55 billion in defense expenditures on hold as a result of more rigorous contract auditing, to the development of a comprehensive guide on servicing and collecting all government direct loans and accounts receivable.

## CONGRESS AND THE BUDGET

Congress has played an important role in reforming decisionmaking processes by developing a budget system that forces competing decision systems to work together. Many have long criticized the way Congress prepares the federal budget, particularly for being uncoordinated. There is no congressional unit responsible for keeping national priorities in perspective when budgetary decisions are made that affect broader economic policy. Another complaint has been over legislation containing entitlement programs, which put almost three-fourths of federal spending outside of congressional control. Critics also deplore the perennial disruption of executive branch operations when Congress fails to pass appropriations bills before a new fiscal year begins.

Perhaps the greatest reform efforts have been made by members of Congress themselves, motivated by the longtime inclination of presidents to usurp their traditional powers. This conflict acquired new intensity in the early 1970s when President Nixon impounded congressionally appropriated funds in his effort to control federal spending. When Nixon challenged Congress to limit spending in FY 1973 to $250 billion, many members agreed on the ceiling figure but felt strongly that they, not the president, should decide how the money was allocated. A Joint Study Committee on Budget Control was created and instructed to find ways of increasing congressional control over the budgetary process. The result of the committee's work, and of subsequent hearings and debate, was the Congressional Budget and Impoundment Control Act of 1974.

The act brought about these major changes in congressional institutions, procedures, and timetables for handling budgetary matters:

1. New budget committees were established in the House and Senate.
2. The Congressional Budget Office (CBO) was created.
3. Congress instructed itself to make coordinated overall decisions on revenue and spending relationships before making individual revenue or appropriations decisions.
4. A revised budget timetable was established.
5. The role of the General Accounting Office (GAO) in providing budget-related information was strengthened.

6.  More information was to be required from the executive branch.
7.  Anti-impoundment laws were strengthened.[9]

The budget committees now play a crucial role in the process. After receiving budget requests from the executive branch and analytical reports from other congressional units, by mid-April the budget committees "must, within a rigid time schedule, establish a congressional position in subsequent consideration and passage of appropriations and other legislation."[10] These goals are communicated to the various appropriations committees through a concurrent resolution. The appropriations committees then report on their spending bills, which are reviewed by the budget committees. Finally, the budget committees issue a second concurrent resolution that essentially sets a final budget ceiling; it informs the appropriations committees of the dollar adjustments that must be made in their spending bills. These changes are made by late September, approximately one week before the new fiscal year begins on October 1.

Has congressional budget reform been a success? The answer depends, of course, on the criteria for success. Various people supported the act for different and conflicting reasons. Political scientists John Ellwood and James A. Thurber suggest that a broad coalition of support ensured a solid majority in favor of budget reform:

> Both conservatives who wanted to cut spending and liberal Democrats who wanted to increase spending and change priorities saw the reform as a means to achieve their ends. . . . The reform was supported by members who saw the elimination of back-door and uncontrollable spending as a first step toward allowing greater short-term congressional control over the budget, and by members who felt that the only way to achieve congressional budget control was some form of forward planning and/or advanced budgeting.[11]

The success of the act should not be judged by specific policy outcomes—more for butter and less for guns, or vice versa. The act's greatest value may lie in the methodological assistance it gives the political process in setting policy priorities. According to one expert, "staff members in both Budget Committees and the Congressional Budget Office report noticing a change in the awareness and understanding of legislators [of budget and priorities issues] ."[12]

In this respect, congressional budget reform is similar to the management reform measures discussed above. None of these reforms overlook the fact that ours is a diverse society, inhabited by people with a wide variety of frequently conflicting interests. The purpose of each reform, however, is to encourage our political and government institutions to consider alternative policies and their consequences intelligently and, most important, to make their final decisions more explicit and thus more open to public scrutiny.

While the budget act worked reasonably well in the 1970s, the process began to unravel during the Reagan administration. The movement for a balanced budget, brought on by increased budget deficits, caused many members of Congress to harden their positions on the funding of new programs and the extension of existing ones. The result was a legislative stalemate on both substantive and procedural issues. These delays made it virtually impossible for Congress to complete its work on the federal budget according to the timetable established in the budget act. Consequently, Congress was able to pass only one federal budget between the fiscal years of 1982 and 1986. In previous years continuing resolutions had been passed that permitted government agencies to continue operating in the next fiscal year on essentially the same appropriations they had received in the preceding year.

President Reagan and many members of both houses of Congress have supported a balanced budget amendment to the Constitution. There have never been sufficient votes, however, to pass such an amendment. During the early 1980s, when discussion of a balanced budget amendment was commonplace, the federal budget deficit continued to grow from $100 billion to more than $211 billion in FY 1985. President Reagan, a strong proponent of balancing the federal budget, has yet to submit to Congress a balanced budget.

Partially in response to that failure but also out of the frustration of trying to reconcile the differences between defense and domestic program spending, Congress enacted one of the most important pieces of budget legislation in history, at the end of the 1985 session. The Balanced Budget and Emergency Deficit Control Act—sometimes referred to as Gramm-Rudman-Hollings after the three senators who authored it—triggers automatic spending cuts if Congress and the president are unable to meet the specified deficit targets agreed upon in the legislation. In other words, if Congress and the president do not take the necessary action to meet the deficit targets, spending cuts will be made automatically according to a formula and by a specific date.

The new budget process begins earlier; in 1987 the president is scheduled to submit his budget on January 5. All other dates in the budget process are also moved forward so that the Office of Management and Budget and the Congressional Budget Office can make their budget deficit projections for the next fiscal year by August 20. If these projections indicate a deficit of more than $10 billion above target, the president can issue an executive order that will cut spending enough to achieve the targeted deficit figure. Congress then has one month to develop an alternate plan and to enact legislation implementing it. On October 15 the president must issue his final order reducing federal spending enough to comply with the deficit targets in the law.

The current deficit targets represent a real challenge to both the president and Congress. The law requires the following maximum deficits: FY 1987, $144 billion; FY 1988, $108 billion; FY 1989, $72 billion; FY 1990, $36 billion; and FY 1991, balanced budget.

The budget act requires that if the president and Congress cannot reduce spending to the target figures, all automatically triggered spending cuts must be divided evenly between defense and domestic programs. Several programs are exempt from the automatic cut provisions: Social Security, Medicaid, Aid to Families with Dependent Children, nutrition programs, Supplemental Security Income, food stamps, veterans' compensation and pensions, and interest on the national debt.

Government efforts to improve management and create centralized institutions have been somewhat successful. Nevertheless, the government programs handled by small decision systems remain the best managed. If a program fits neatly into one or a few closely related decisionmaking systems, the chances are good that government will process that program effectively. If a program does not fit into a decisionmaking system, it is likely to be chaotically managed and to produce unpredictable results.

But those who characterize all government decisionmaking systems as irrational, wasteful, overlapping, and excessively deliberative are missing an important point. Public decisionmaking systems function in the same way that a democratic government processes issues. Competition among government decisionmakers may lead to duplication of efforts and uncoordinated administration, yet these are the basic characteristics of free enterprise and decentralized control of government. This type of management may be wasteful, but too much coordination has the effect of centralizing government power, perhaps dangerously so. This paradox is the dilemma—the rock and the hard place—of government in a democracy.

## NOTES

1. Charles E. Lindblom, "The Science of 'Muddling Through'," *Public Administration Review* 19 (1959): 79–99.

2. Ibid., p. 89.

3. Herbert Kaufman, *Are Government Organizations Immortal?* (Washington, D.C.: The Brookings Institution, 1976), p. 34.

4. There is some difference of opinion as to whether the deficit creation/control strategy was deliberately planned and pursued by President Reagan and his advisors, or was accidental. In either case, it was effective and had the result the president wanted. See Tom Wicker, "A Deliberate Deficit," *New York Times*, 19 July 1985, and Daniel Patrick Moynihan, "Reagan's Inflate-the-Deficit Game," *New York Times*, 21 July 1985.

5. Transcript, "Face the Nation," CBS–TV, 9 July 1978, pp. 15–16. Used with permission.

6. President Reagan established the commission in Executive Order No. 12369, 30 June 1982. For an abbreviated version of the Commission's findings, see J. Peter Grace, *War on Waste* (New York: Macmillan Publishing Company, 1984).

7. Congressional Budget Office and General Accounting Office, *Analysis of the Grace Commission's Major Proposals for Cost Control* (Washington, D.C.: U.S. Government Printing Office, 1984).

8. Executive Office of the President, Office of Management and Budget, *Management of the U.S. Government, Fiscal Year 1987.*

9. James J. Finley, "The 1974 Congressional Initiative in Budget Making," *Public Administration Review* 35 (1975): 272.

10. Ibid.

11. John Ellwood and James A. Thurber, "The New Congressional Budget Process: The Hows and Whys of House-Senate Differences," in Lawrence C. Dodd and Bruce I. Oppenheimer, *Congress Reconsidered*, 2d ed. (Washington, D.C.: Congressional Quarterly Press, 1981), pp. 247–51.

12. Lance T. LeLoup, *Budgetary Politics: Dollars, Deficits, Decisions* (Brunswick, Ohio: King's Court Communications, 1977), p. 235.

# 10 BUSINESS AND GOVERNMENT IN THE FUTURE

The future is likely to require more cooperation between corporate executives and government, not less. Some indications of this trend include: the continuing expansion of the federal government's role in the economy; public concern about the effects of deregulation and unabated public support for government benefits; and appeals for government intervention to reverse the imbalance in U.S. foreign trade.

The U.S. government has continued to spend an increasing proportion of the GNP, despite the dogged efforts of a conservative and enormously popular president to reverse that trend. Public opinion seems to be increasingly suspicious of big business and wary of deregulation. In fact, calls for more regulation of banking, financial markets, and airline safety are not uncommon. There is growing interest in the "public goods" provided by government, such as a cleaner environment and state-supported education. The nation's competitive position in world trade has slipped badly in recent years, and still appears to be declining. There is increasing pressure on government to take steps to halt this trend.

The agendas of corporate stockholders contain more social issues than ever before.[1] On the other hand, issues that concern business—many of which, like tax reform, split business support in different directions—are appearing with greater frequency on the government's agenda. The tax reform of 1986 represents a significant reduction of government's role in the economy. One would have thought business would strongly support the proposed reforms. Not so. Jeffrey Birnbaum of the *Wall Street Journal* put it succinctly: "General Motors Corp. likes tax overhaul. Ford Motor Co. doesn't. The U.S. Chamber of Commerce wants to kill the legislation. The National Federation of Independent Business is working hard to get it passed."[2]

Business interest in government policy and operations remains strong, if tax reform politics are any measure. The new tax law, which eliminates an estimated $40 billion in write-offs for business, could intensify pressure on government to either create other types of benefits for business or restore the advantages taken away in 1986.[3]

In the 1970s and early 1980s, corporate and government leaders tried to make the public and private sectors more autonomous, but those efforts seem to have failed. The present level of business-government interaction—cooperative at times and conflicting at others—will endure for some time.

## AN EXPANDING FEDERAL ROLE
## IN THE ECONOMY

Richard Nixon came into the presidency dedicated to reducing the role of the federal government in the lives of citizens. This has been a common theme with all his successors. Nixon wanted to transfer to state and local officials more authority and responsibility for program initiation, funding, and management. He hoped to accomplish this goal through a program called New Federalism, the cornerstone of his domestic policy. The record shows, however, that nothing came of Nixon's efforts. In 1969 federal grants to state and local governments amounted to $20.3 billion. Five years later, when Nixon resigned from office, federal grants had more than doubled to $43.4 billion, averaging about 20 percent growth per year.[4]

Ronald Reagan has made more ambitious and eloquent statements about the need to reduce federal control and funding of domestic programs by returning even more program authority to the states. Like Nixon, Reagan called his program New Federalism; like its predecessor, modern New Federalism has achieved only marginal gains. During the Reagan administration the number of federal grants has been reduced through consolidation, but the total funding figure continues to increase, albeit at a slower rate than in the Nixon, Ford, and Carter years.

Reagan has eliminated some domestic programs, such as the Youth Conservation Corps, public service jobs, and regional development commissions. But many other programs have survived repeated attempts to eliminate them. Some of the persistent survivors are the Small Business Administration, Amtrak, urban development action grants, community services block grants, the Legal Services Corporation, and the Economic Development Administration. In a few cases the Reagan administration was successful in cutting back programs to a lower level. Some programs cut back in 1981 and 1982, however, received funding increases in 1984 and 1985. These include Elementary and Secondary Education Act programs, some social services programs (Head Start, Older Americans Act), and Pell college scholarship grants.[5] Even a president as popular as Ronald Reagan has had no remarkable permanent victories in the battle to reverse the upward trend of government spending.

One of the most significant Reagan administration failures is the continuing inability to reduce the growth in federal government expenditures as a portion of GNP. Reducing the government's role in the economy was a frequently stated goal of Reagan as a candidate and then as president. Not only has his administration fallen far short of this goal, but in fact it has presided over a growth in federal spending that has exceeded the inflation rate. In 1980 federal spending accounted for about 22.5 percent of GNP; in FY 1986 this figure had risen to 25 percent. Instead of being cut, federal spending has been rearranged. Defense and social security, the two largest items in the federal budget for several years, now receive even larger appropriations while some other programs receive much less. Despite these rearrangements, the basic patterns of government expenditure remain intact.[6] If this can be said toward the end of the second term of a popular conservative president, it is very unlikely that drastic changes will be made anytime soon in federal government spending patterns, and in expenditures as a percentage of GNP.

## FIFTEEN YEARS OF DEREGULATION

The extent of economic deregulation in the last fifteen years has been remarkable. The major deregulation activities over that period (see Table 3-2) reflect a shift away from the belief that government policies could improve economic efficiency and productivity or correct inequities created by markets.

Deregulation began as a series of academic exercises to demonstrate some of the inequities produced by regulation. Licensing and market entry restrictions, for example, limited competition and artificially forced prices up. Regulation was thus identified as one of the reasons for decreased productivity and slower economic growth.

There are signs, however, that the extensive deregulation activities of the past several years may not be sustainable. A student of regulatory politics has noted that "the history of economic *regulation* is a history of a belief in governmental action to correct perceived deficiencies of the market. The history of *deregulation* is a history of challenges to that belief."[7] Any further deregulation, and maintaining deregulatory accomplishments to date, will depend upon the public's opinion of the efficacy and fairness of these measures.

There are indications of public dissatisfaction with airline and telephone deregulation. Economically, these misgivings are probably misplaced, but nevertheless they exist and may grow stronger. Airline deregulation has led to the creation of more than twice as many airlines and the scheduling of many more flights than ever before; but the number of federal safety inspectors has not kept pace with the increased frequency of flights. Also, when airlines are cutting fares to compete for new passengers, air traffic safety may be endangered. Although there is no statistical evidence that airlines are cutting corners on safety, there is some empirical evidence. In 1985 the Federal Aviation Agency fined American Airlines $1.5 million for safety offenses, and in 1986 attempted to collect $9.5 million from Eastern Airlines for 8,000 alleged safety violations. (Eastern has refused to pay and is appealing the ruling.) John O'Brien, safety director of the Airline Pilots' Association, told a congressional committee, "All too often safety is losing out to cost cutting."[8]

Public skepticism of banking deregulation is also growing, at least in some parts of the country. The banking system is sound, as is the airline travel system. Yet those who bank in some of the midwestern farm states (and in Maryland) had their confidence shaken when several banks and thrift institutions failed. With or without justification, the public seems to be questioning the wisdom and extent of recent economic deregulation, and probably would not support any more such activity at this time.

Business should be concerned about the public's attitude; public confidence in business itself is not high. Even as a probusiness president has disparaged public-sector performance by comparing it unfavorably with business, business has not gained in popularity. About 25 percent of those polled by the Roper Organization in 1983–85 responded with an unfavorable view of large corporations. This may have been a slight improvement over earlier polls, yet when asked a series of six specific questions about aspects of business like profits and power, the public responds much more negatively than in the past. Antibusiness opinion has hovered at about 60 percent for more than a decade. Further corroboration of antibusiness sentiment surfaced in the results of polling done after President Reagan introduced his sweeping tax reform proposal. The polls revealed that the single most popular feature of the proposal was shifting tax burdens from individuals to corporations. Seven out of eight of those interviewed endorsed this component of the tax reform plan.[9]

At the same time, the public does not seem to have lost interest in maintaining social and environmental programs at or near their current levels. A *Los Angeles Times* poll in February 1986 discovered that 61 percent of those polled did not want to eliminate student loan programs; 71 percent did not want to cut back on farm subsidies; and 73 percent did not want to eliminate the Small Business Administration.[10]

## PROTECTIONISM AND INDUSTRIAL POLICY

The large merchandise trade deficit—nearly $150 billion in 1985— has invoked demands from some quarters for protectionist measures and calls for more systematic government industrial policies from others. The trade deficit more than quadrupled from 1982 to 1986, partly because of the high value of the dollar. By contrast, the 1971 current account balance was in surplus by over $6 billion.

As the dollar started to decline in early 1986, some of the pressure on government to take protectionist measures began to subside because the devalued dollar could result in increased U.S. exports. Nevertheless, the most far-reaching general trade protection bill introduced in recent years passed the House of Representatives in April 1986 by a very large vote.

Several reasons other than the high value of the dollar are also given for the trade deficit. They include low worker productivity in the United States, high wages, barriers to U.S. products abroad, "dumping" of foreign products in the U.S. market, and the high levels of debt in the third world. Imposing higher tariffs on imported products and other retaliatory measures taken by the U.S. government are risky and probably harmful responses. But whether the response is restricting imports or improving the competitiveness of U.S. exports in international markets, these policies, and the business community's contribution to developing them, will be critical issues in the next several years.

The 1986 Omnibus Trade Bill (H.R. 4800) includes a provision that would create a commission responsible for evaluating the existing programs and laws that encourage or otherwise affect U.S. industrial competitiveness. The purpose of this provision is to develop a more positive strategy for dealing with the trade deficit. The representative behind this proposal, John J. LaFalce (D-NY), sees it as a way of dealing with trade deficits without resorting to portectionism.[11]

The 1986 trade bill did not become law, but high-level interest in developing strategies to improve U.S. competitiveness seems to be increasing. The undersecretary of commerce for international trade concluded in a recent report:

> To survive and prosper in an increasingly competitive global economy, it is essential that . . . the dollar decline in value . . . (and that) we accelerate actions to minimize the impediments to mobility of capital, know-how, and labor. . . . We should implement a strategy that encourages American business to produce and export from America.[12]

Today corporations are spending millions of dollars each year to identify and monitor public policy issues of interest to them. The Conference Board, a research organization that analyzes public policy issues for business, surveyed its members in 1986 on the most important public policy issues affecting them and on the extent of their involvement in those issues. The answers from over 250 corporations reflect the range of issues confronting decisionmakers in Washington.[13] The ten issues cited most often, in order of importance, were:

1. The federal budget deficit and related tax reform
2. Regulatory reform
3. Environmental protection
4. Energy development

5.  International trade relations
6.  Health care cost containment
7.  Economic concentration
8.  Local issues
9.  South African investment
10.  Plant closing laws

A surprisingly large number of firms are either "actively involved in" or "closely monitoring" current public policy issues. This is how nearly 75 percent of the firms surveyed by the Conference Board describe their participation in budget and tax proposals (see Table 10–1). Nearly the same level of interest is reported in more than a dozen other policy areas. The Conference Board data reflect industry's growing concern and involvement in public policy. Given the long-term nature of these issues, business involvement in public policy is unlikely to slacken in the future.

Predicting the future for business–government relations is an uncertain task at best. Looking at the experience of the past several years, and attempting to foresee the next few, we conclude that the mutual dependence of business and government will probably not diminish and is in fact likely to grow.

The public now seems to expect government and business to collaborate, and appears to be comfortable with the degree of interaction that has prevailed over the last several decades. The successful business executives will continue to be those who understand government and how it affects the economy in general and their corporations in particular. Understanding and participating effectively in government decision processes are management skills that are bound to become increasingly valued in the corporate world.

**Table 10-1.** Levels of Corporate Involvement in Public Policy Issues.

| Title of Issue | Percent of Firms Actively Involved | Percent of Firms Closely Monitoring | Percent of Firms Reporting General Interest |
|---|---|---|---|
| Federal budget deficit or tax reform | 50.6 | 23.0 | 25.1 |
| Environmental protection | 46.9 | 24.3 | 20.2 |
| Regulatory reform | 41.6 | 25.5 | 30.0 |
| Health care costs | 41.2 | 37.0 | 18.1 |
| International trade | 35.8 | 21.8 | 27.2 |
| Reregulation | 31.5 | 31.1 | 29.5 |
| Local community issues | 29.5 | 23.7 | 35.3 |
| Business and education | 21.0 | 19.8 | 45.7 |
| Electoral reform | 20.2 | 43.2 | 29.2 |
| Financial disclosure | 19.8 | 42.8 | 30.5 |
| Plant closing laws | 19.8 | 33.7 | 29.2 |
| Comparable worth | 15.2 | 50.6 | 30.0 |
| Age discrimination | 14.8 | 53.5 | 29.2 |
| Economic concentration | 14.8 | 43.2 | 37.0 |
| International investment | 14.0 | 24.0 | 32.2 |
| South Africa investment | 12.5 | 13.8 | 19.2 |
| Discrimination against handicapped | 12.4 | 36.8 | 46.3 |

| | | | |
|---|---|---|---|
| Ethnic discrimination | 10.7 | 48.8 | 36.8 |
| Family services | 7.9 | 25.7 | 54.8 |
| Structural unemployment | 7.9 | 16.7 | 55.8 |
| Employment-at-will | 7.8 | 41.2 | 41.2 |
| Federal Reserve issues | 6.2 | 26.9 | 53.3 |
| Third World issues | 4.6 | 13.3 | 19.9 |
| Religion and business | 4.1 | 15.6 | 36.2 |
| Immigration reform | 2.9 | 10.3 | 34.2 |
| Aid to Israel | 0.8 | 4.6 | 20.7 |
| Disarmament negotiations | 0.8 | 2.5 | 23.9 |

Source: Catherine Morrison, *Forecasting Public Affairs Priorities*, Research Bulletin No. 192 (New York: The Conference Board, 1986), p. 5.

## NOTES

1.  Barnaby J. Feder, "Annual Meetings: Surge of Social Issues," *New York Times*, 15 April 1986.
2.  Jeffrey H. Birnbaum, "Business's Schism Over Tax Overhaul Reflects the Divide-and-Conquer Strategy of Proponents," *Wall Street Journal*, 5 December 1985.
3.  Paul Blustein, "U.S. Business Finds 40 Billion Reasons to Back Senate Committee's Tax Bill Over House Version," *Wall Street Journal*, 6 June 1986.
4.  U.S. Advisory Commission on Intergovernmental Relations, *Significant Features of Fiscal Federalism, 1985.*
5.  Paul Blustein, "Recent Budget Battles Leave the Basic Tenets of the Welfare State Intact," *Wall Street Journal*, 21 October 1985.
6.  Robert D. Hershey, Jr., "Spending Rose Sharply in 'Reagan Revolution'," *New York Times*, 2 February 1986.
7.  James D. Carroll, speech at the Brookings Institution, National Issues Forum, "A Decade of Economic Deregulation: Assessing the Results," Washington, D.C., April 11, 1986.
8.  Quoted in Tom Wicker, "What Price Safety?" *New York Times*, 25 March 1986.
9.  William Schneider, "Public Tells Business, 'You've Got Enough'," *National Journal*, 13 July 1985.
10.  Cited in "Opinion Outlook." *National Journal*, 7 June 1986. For a further elaboration of these popular views, see also Thomas Ferguson and Joel Rodgers, "The Myth of America's Turn to the Right," *Atlantic*, May 1986.
11.  Congressman LaFalce is chairman of the U.S. House Subcommittee on Economic Stabilization. He has articulated this position often.
12.  Department of Commerce, International Trade Commission, *U.S. Manufacturing at a Crossroads: Surviving and Prospering in a More Competitive Global Economy*, by Lionel H. Olmer, 14 June 1985, pp. vii–viii.
13.  Catherine Morrison, *Forecasting Public Affairs Priorities*, Research Bulletin No. 192 (New York: The Conference Board, 1986), pp. 3–6.

# APPENDIXES

# HOW A BILL BECOMES LAW

## Introduction of Bills

A House member (including the resident commissioner of Puerto Rico and non-voting delegates of the District of Columbia, Guam, the Virgin Islands, and American Samoa) may introduce any one of several types of bills and resolutions by handing it to the clerk of the House or placing it in a box called the hopper. A senator first gains recognition of the presiding officer to announce the introduction of a bill. If objection is offered by any senator the introduction of the bill is postponed until the following day.

As the next step in either the House or Senate, the bill is numbered, referred to the appropriate committee, labeled with the sponsor's name; and sent to the Government Printing Office so that copies can be made for subsequent study and action. Senate bills may be jointly sponsored and carry several senators' names. Until 1978, the House limited the number of members who could co-sponsor any one bill; the ceiling was eliminated at the beginning of the 96th Congress. A bill written in the Executive Branch and proposed as an administration measure usually is introduced by the chairman of the congressional committee which has jurisdiction.

**Bills** — Prefixed with "HR" in the House, "S" in the Senate, followed by a number. Used as the form for most legislation, whether general or special, public or private.

**Joint Resolutions**—Designated H J Res or S J Res. Subject to the same procedure as bills, with the exception of a joint resolution proposing an amendment to the Constitution. The latter must be approved by two-thirds of both houses and is thereupon sent directly to the administrator of general services for submission to the states for ratification rather than being presented to the president for his approval.

**Concurrent Resolutions**—Designated H Con Res or S Con Res. Used for matters affecting the operations of both houses. These resolutions do not become law.

**Resolutions**—Designated H Res or S Res. Used for a matter concerning the operation of either house alone and adopted only by the chamber in which it originates.

## Committee Action

A bill is referred to the appropriate committee by a House parliamentarian on the Speaker's order, or by the Senate president. Sponsors may indicate their preferences for referral, although custom and chamber rule generally govern. An exception is the referral of private bills, which are sent to whatever group is designated by their sponsors. Bills are technically considered "read for the first time" when referred to House committees.

When a bill reaches a committee it is placed upon the group's calendar. At that time it comes under the sharpest congressional focus. Its chances for passage are quickly determined—and the great majority of bills fall by the legislative roadside. Failure of a committee to act on a bill is equivalent to killing it; the measure can be withdrawn from the group's purview only by a discharge petition signed by a majority of the House membership on House bills, or by adoption of a special resolution in the Senate. Discharge attempts rarely succeed.

The first committee action taken on a bill usually is a request for comment on it by interested agencies of the government. The committee chairman may assign the bill to a subcommittee for study and hearings, or it may be considered by the full committee. Hearings may be public, closed (executive session), or both. A subcommittee, after considering a bill, reports to the full committee its recommendations for action and any proposed amendments.

The full committee then votes on its recommendation to the House or Senate. This procedure is called "ordering a bill reported." Occasionally a committee may order a bill reported unfavorably; most of the time a report, submitted by the chairman of the committee to the House or Senate, calls for favorable action on the measure since the committee can effectively "kill" a bill by simply failing to take any action.

When a committee sends a bill to the chamber floor, it explains its reasons in a written statement, called a report, which accompanies the bill. Often committee members opposing a measure issue dissenting minority statements which are included in the report.

Usually, the committee "marks up" or proposes amendments to the bill. If they are substantial and the measure is complicated, the committee may order a "clean bill" introduced, which will embody the proposed amendments. The original bill then is put aside and the "clean bill," with a new number, is reported to the floor.

The chamber must approve, alter, or reject the committee amendments before the bill itself can be put to a vote.


### Floor Action

After a bill is reported back to the house where it originated, it is placed on the calendar.

There are five legislative calendars in the House, issued in one cumulative calendar titled *Calendars of the United States House of Representatives and History of Legislation.* The House calendars are:

The *Union Calendar* to which are referred bills raising revenues, general appropriation bills and any measures directly or indirectly appropriating money or property. It is the Calendar of the Committee of the Whole House on the State of the Union.

The *House Calendar* to which are referred bills of a public character not raising revenue or appropriating money or property.

The *Consent Calendar* to which are referred bills of a non-controversial nature that are passed without debate when the Consent Calendar is called on the first and third Mondays of each month.

The *Private Calendar* to which are referred bills for relief in the nature of claims against the United States or private immigration bills that are passed without debate when the Private Calendar is called the first and third Tuesdays of each month.

The *Discharge Calendar* to which are referred motions to discharge committees when the necessary signatures are signed to a discharge petition.

There is only one legislative calendar in the Senate and one "executive calendar" for treaties and nominations submitted to the Senate. When the Senate Calendar is called, each senator is limited to five minutes debate on each bill.

*Debate.* A bill is brought to debate by varying procedures. If a routine measure, it may await the call of the calendar. If it is urgent or important, it can be taken up in the Senate either by unanimous consent or by a majority vote. The policy committee of the majority party in the Senate schedules the bills that it wants taken up for debate.

In the House, precedence is granted if a special rule is obtained from the Rules Committee. A request for a special rule is usually made by the chairman of the committee that favorably reported the bill, supported by the bill's sponsor and other committee members. The request, considered by the Rules Committee in the same fashion that other committees consider legislative measures, is in the form of a resolution providing for immediate consideration of the bill. The Rules Committee reports the resolution to the House where it is debated and voted upon in the same fashion as regular bills. If the Rules Committee should fail to report a rule requested by a committee, there are several ways to bring the bill to the House floor — under suspension of the rules, on Calendar Wednesday, or by a discharge motion.

The resolutions providing special rules are important because they specify how long the bill may be debated and whether it may be amended from the floor. If floor amendments are banned, the bill is considered under a "closed rule," which permits only members of the committee that first reported the measure to the House to alter its language, subject to chamber acceptance.

When a bill is debated under an "open rule," amendments may be offered from the floor. Committee amendments are always taken up first, but may be changed, as may all amendments up to the second degree, i.e., an amendment to an amendment to an amendment is not in order.

Duration of debate in the House depends on whether the bill is under discussion by the House proper or before the House when it is sitting as the Committee of the Whole House on the State of the Union. In the former, the amount of time for debate is determined either by special rule or is allocated with an hour for each member if the measure is under consideration without a rule. In the Committee of the Whole the amount of time agreed on for general debate is equally divided between proponents and opponents. At the end of general discussion, the bill is read section by section for amendment. Debate on an amendment is limited to five minutes for each side.

Senate debate is usually unlimited. It can be halted only by unanimous consent by "cloture," which requires a three-fifths majority of the entire Senate except for proposed changes in the Senate rules. The latter requires a two-thirds vote.

The House sits as the Committee of the Whole when it considers any tax measure or bill dealing with public appropriations. It can also resolve itself into the Committee of the Whole if a member moves to do so and the motion is carried. The Speaker appoints a member to serve as the chairman. The rules of the House permit the Committee of the Whole to meet with any 100 members on the floor, and to amend and act on bills with a quorum of the 100, within the time limitations mentioned previously. When the Committee of the Whole has acted, it "rises," the Speaker returns as the presiding officer of the House and the member appointed chairman of the Committee of the Whole reports the action of the committee and its recommendations (amendments adopted).

*Votes.*  Voting on bills may occur repeatedly before they are finally approved or rejected. The House votes on the rule for the bill and on various amendments to the bill. Voting on amendments often is a more illuminating test of a bill's support than is the final tally. Sometimes members approve final passage of bills after vigorously supporting amendments which, if adopted, would have scuttled the legislation.

The Senate has three different methods of voting: an untabulated voice vote, a standing vote (called a division) and a recorded roll call to which members answer "yea" or "nay" when their names are called. The House also employs voice and standing votes, but since January 1973 yeas and nays have been recorded by an electronic voting device, eliminating the need for time-consuming roll calls.

Another method of voting, used in the House only, is the teller vote. Traditionally, members filed up the center aisle past counters; only vote totals were announced. Since 1971, one-fifth of a quorum can demand that the votes of individual members be recorded, thereby forcing them to take a public position on amendments to key bills. Electronic voting now is commonly used for this purpose.

After amendments to a bill have been voted upon, a vote may be taken on a motion to recommit the bill to committee. If carried, this vote removes the bill from the chamber's calendar. If the motion is unsuccessful, the bill then is "read for the third time." An actual reading usually is dispensed with. Until 1965, an opponent of a bill could delay this move by objecting and asking for a full reading of an engrossed (certified in final firm) copy of the bill. After the "third reading," the vote on final passage is taken.

The final vote may be followed by a motion to reconsider, and this motion itself may be followed by a move to lay the motion on the table. Usually, those voting for the bill's passage vote for the tabling motion, thus safeguarding the final passage action. With that, the bill has been formally passed by the chamber. While a motion to reconsider a Senate vote is pending on a bill, the measure cannot be sent to the House.

### Action in Second House

After a bill is passed it is sent to the other chamber. This body may then take one of several steps. It may pass the bill as is—accepting the other chamber's language. It may send the bill to committee for scrutiny or alteration, or reject the entire bill, advising the other house of its actions. Or it may simply ignore the bill submitted while it continues work on its own version of the proposed legislation. Frequently, one chamber may approve a version of a bill that is greatly at variance with the version already passed by the other house, and then substitute its amendments for the language of the other, retaining only the latter's bill designation.

A provision of the Legislative Reorganization Act of 1970 permits a separate House vote on any non-germane amendment added by the Senate to a House-passed bill and requires a majority vote to retain the amendment. Previously the House was forced to act on the bill, as a whole; the only way to defeat the non-germane amendment was to reject the entire bill.

Often the second chamber makes only minor changes. If these are readily agreed to by the other house, the bill then is routed to the White House for signing. However, if the opposite chamber basically alters the bill submitted to it the measure usually is "sent to conference." The chamber that has possession of the "papers" (engrossed bill, engrossed amendments, messages of transmittal) requests a conference and the other chamber must agree to it. If the second house does not agree, the bill dies.

### Conference, Final Action

*Conference.* A conference undertakes to harmonize conflicting House and Senate versions of a legislative bill. The conference is usually staffed by senior members (conferees), appointed by the presiding officers of the two houses, from the committees that managed the bills. Under this arrangement the conferees of one house have the duty of trying to maintain their chamber's position in the face of amending actions by the conferees (also referred to as "managers") of the other house.

The number of conferees from each chamber may vary, the range usually being from three to nine members in each group, depending upon the length or complexity of the bill involved. There may be five representatives and three senators on the conference committee, or the reverse. But a majority vote controls the action of each group so that a larger representation does not give one chamber a voting advantage over the other chamber's conferees.

Theoretically, conferees are not allowed to write new legislation in reconciling the two versions before them, but this curb sometimes is bypassed. Many bills have been put into acceptable compromise form only after new language was provided by the conferees. The 1970 Reorganization Act attempted to tighten restrictions on conferees by forbidding them to introduce any language on a topic that neither chamber sent to conference or to modify any topic beyond the scope of the different House and Senate versions.

Frequently, the ironing out of difficulties takes days or even weeks. Conferences on involved appropriation bills sometimes are particularly drawn out.

Figure A-1.  How a Bill Becomes Law.

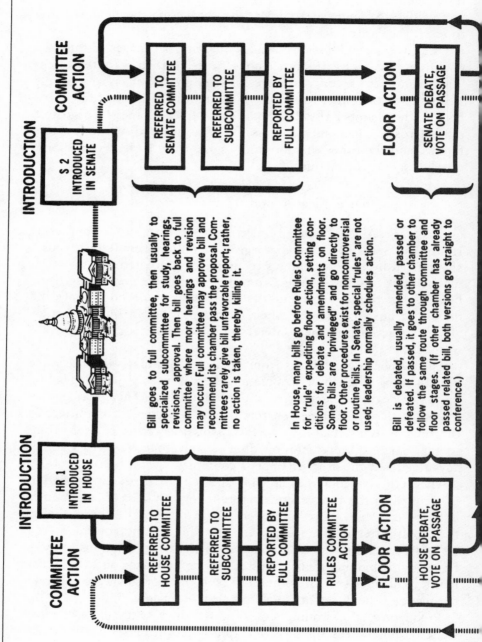

**INTRODUCTION**

**HR 1 INTRODUCED IN HOUSE**

**S 2 INTRODUCED IN SENATE**

**COMMITTEE ACTION**

REFERRED TO HOUSE COMMITTEE

REFERRED TO SUBCOMMITTEE

REPORTED BY FULL COMMITTEE

RULES COMMITTEE ACTION

REFERRED TO SENATE COMMITTEE

REFERRED TO SUBCOMMITTEE

REPORTED BY FULL COMMITTEE

**FLOOR ACTION**

HOUSE DEBATE, VOTE ON PASSAGE

SENATE DEBATE, VOTE ON PASSAGE

Bill goes to full committee, then usually to specialized subcommittee for study, hearings, revisions, approval. Then bill goes back to full committee where more hearings and revision may occur. Full committee may approve bill and recommend its chamber pass the proposal. Committees rarely give bill unfavorable report; rather, no action is taken, thereby killing it.

In House, many bills go before Rules Committee for "rule" expediting floor action, setting conditions for debate and amendments on floor. Some bills are "privileged" and go directly to floor. Other procedures exist for noncontroversial or routine bills. In Senate, special "rules" are not used; leadership normally schedules action.

Bill is debated, usually amended, passed or defeated. If passed, it goes to other chamber to follow the same route through committee and floor stages. (If other chamber has already passed related bill, both versions go straight to conference.)

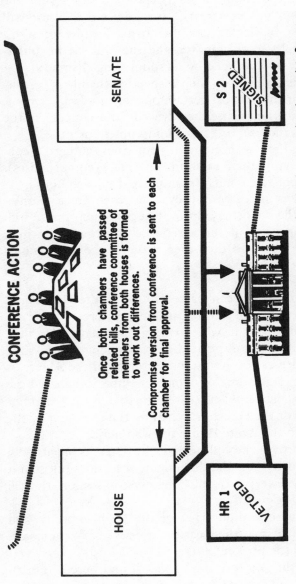

## CONFERENCE ACTION

Once both chambers have passed related bills, conference committee of members from both houses is formed to work out differences.

Compromise version from conference is sent to each chamber for final approval.

SENATE

HOUSE

S 2

SIGNED

HR 1

VETOED

**Compromise version approved by both houses is sent to President who can either sign it into law or veto it and return it to Congress. Congress may override veto by a two-thirds majority vote in both houses; bill then becomes law without President's signature.**

This graphic shows the most typical way in which proposed legislation is enacted into law. There are more complicated, as well as simpler, routes, and most bills fall by the wayside and never become law. The process is illustrated with two hypothetical bills, House bill No. 1 (HR 1) and Senate bill No. 2 (S 2). Each bill must be passed by both houses of Congress in identical form before it can become law. The path of HR 1 is traced by a solid line, that of S 2 by a broken line. However, in practice most legislation begins as similar proposals in both houses.

As a conference proceeds, conferees reconcile differences between the versions, but generally they grant concessions only insofar as they remain sure that the chamber they represent will accept the compromises. Occasionally, uncertainty over how either house will react, or the positive refusal of a chamber to back down on a disputed amendment, results in an impasse, and the bills die in conference even though each was approved by its sponsoring chamber.

Conferees sometimes go back to their respective chambers for further instructions, when they report certain portions in disagreement. Then the chamber concerned can either "recede and concur" in the amendment of the other house, or "insist on its amendment."

When the conferees have reached agreement, they prepare a conference report embodying their recommendations (compromises). The reports, in document form, must be submitted to each house.

The conference report must be approved by each house. Consequently, approval of the report is approval of the compromise bill. In the order of voting on conference reports, the chamber which asked for a conference yields to the other chamber the opportunity to vote first.

*Final Steps.* After a bill has been passed by both the House and Senate in identical form, all of the original papers are sent to the enrolling clerk of the chamber in which the bill originated. He then prepares an enrolled bill which is printed on parchment paper. When this bill has been certified as correct by the secretary of the Senate or the clerk of the House, depending on which chamber originated the bill, it is signed first (no matter whether it originated in the Senate or House) by the Speaker of the House and then by the president of the Senate. It is next sent to the White House to await action.

If the president approves the bill he signs it, dates it and usually writes the word "approved" on the document. If he does not sign it within 10 days (Sundays excepted) and Congress is in session, the bill becomes law without his signature.

However, should Congress adjourn before the 10 days expire, and the president has failed to sign the measure, it does not become law. This procedure is called the pocket veto.

A president vetoes a bill by refusing to sign it and before the 10-day period expires, returning it to Congress with a message stating his reasons. The message is sent to the chamber which originated the bill.

If no action is taken there on the message, the bill dies. Congress, however, can attempt to override the president's veto and enact the bill, "the objections of the president to the contrary notwithstanding." Overriding of a veto requires a two-thirds vote of those present, who must number a quorum and vote by roll call.

Debate can precede this vote, with motions permitted to lay the message on the table, postpone action on it, or refer it to committee. If the president's veto is overridden by a two-thirds vote in both houses, the bill becomes law. Otherwise it is dead.

When bills are passed finally and signed, or passed over a veto, they are given law numbers in numerical order as they become law. There are two series of numbers, one for public and one for private laws, starting at the number "1" for each two-year term of Congress. They are then identified by law number and by Congress—i.e., Private Law 21, 97th Congress; Public Law 250, 97th Congress (or PL 97–250).

Source: *Current American Government* (Washington, D.C.: Congressional Quarterly Inc., Spring, 1986), pp. 141–44.

# HOW TO USE THE
# *FEDERAL REGISTER*

### What Is the *Federal Register?*

The *Federal Register* is a legal newspaper in which the Executive Department of the United States Government publishes regulations, orders, and other documents. A citizen is thereby informed of his/her rights, his/her obligations, and often, the benefits of his/her Government. The *Register* is issued weekdays by the Office of the Federal Register. It is published in softcover and issues usually run between 150 and 300 pages.

### Who Reads the *Register?*

If you are in business and subject to regulation by a Federal agency, if you are an attorney who might represent a client before a regulatory agency, or if you have a need to know the day-to-day operations of the Federal Government, the *Federal Register* will be useful—even vital—reading for you. There are many other citizens—such as those involved with consumer, conservation, and other special interest groups—who will profit from reading the *Register.*

### How Is the *Register* Organized?

Each issue has five sections: "Presidential Documents," including Executive Orders and Proclamations; "Rules and Regulations," including on occasion policy statements; "Proposed Rules;" "Notices;" and "Sunshine Meetings," including scheduled hearings and meetings open to the public. Each issue has a Selected Subjects finding aid starting on the title page in which a brief statement describes the principal subject of selected documents. A Unified Agenda of Federal Regulations is published in the *Federal Register* every year in October and April as required by Executive Order #12291 of February 17, 1981, and the Regulation Flexibility Act (5 U.S.C. 602).

Anything appearing in the *Register* may be freely copied.

### Is *Register* Information Available in Advance?

Documents are also available for inspection, and may be copied the day before publication in Room 8401, 1100 L Street, N.W., Washington, D.C. *Register* business hours are 8:45 a.m. to 5:15 p.m., Monday through Friday. The office is closed on official holidays.

### Why Is the *Register* Important?

Because advance notice of rulemaking must be given by departments and agencies in the *Register*, citizens can influence the decisionmaking process of the Government. The procedure is simple. An interested individual or organization concerned with a pending regulation may comment on it directly, either in writing, or orally at a hearing, to the office drafting the rule. The comment period varies, but is usually thirty, sixty, or ninety days. In each instance, the *Register* gives detailed instructions on how, when, and where a viewpoint can be expressed.

### Where Is the *Register* Available?

Most public libraries and all Federal Depository Libraries in major cities have copies of the *Federal Register* on file. A sample copy may be obtained by writing the Office of the Federal Register, National Archives and Records Administration, Washington, D.C. 20408, or at GPO bookstores around the nation. Each copy is $1.50; checks or money orders should be made out to the Superintendent of Documents. Subscriptions to the *Federal Register* are $150.00 for six months or $300.00 per year. Write the U.S. Government Printing Office, Washington, D.C. 20402. The *Federal Register* is published by the Office of the Federal Register, National Archives and Records Administration. General Information 202-523-5227.

Source: Office of the Federal Register, Washington, D.C.

# HOW TO USE THE *CODE OF FEDERAL REGULATIONS*

### What Is the *Code of Federal Regulations?*

The *Code of Federal Regulations (CFR)* is a codification of the current general and permanent rules of the various Federal agencies. Name a subject from "air" to "zoological parks" and chances are the *CFR* will contain a regulation about it. All such official regulations are grouped together in the approximately 140 volumes that comprise the *CFR*. The United States is a complex industrial nation and this body of regulations reflects both its size and complexity.

### What Is Its Purpose?

The purpose of the *CFR* is to present the **Complete Text** of agency regulations in one organized publication and to provide a comprehensive and convenient reference for all those who may need to know the text of general and permanent Federal regulations.

### How Is the *Code* Organized?

The *CFR* is organized into fifty Titles representing broad areas subject to regulatory action, for example, Title 20—"Employee Benefits." Each Title is divided into chapters which are assigned to agencies or subagencies issuing regulations pertaining to that broad subject area, for example, Title 20 contains Chapter III—Social Security Administration, Department of Health, Education, and Welfare. Each chapter is divided into parts covering specific functions or programs of the agency. Each part is divided into sections—the basic unit of the *CFR*. Note that some agencies may issue regulations that appear in more than one title, for example, "Trucking" may be subject to rules found both under Title 23—"Highways" and Title 49—"Transportation."

### How Does the *Code* Work?

The *CFR* is keyed to and kept up to date by the daily *Federal Register*. These two publications must be used together to determine the latest version of any given rule. When a Federal agency publishes a regulation in the *Federal Register*, that regulation usually is an amendment to the basic *CFR* in the form of a change, an addition, or a deletion. For a person to research all of the regulations that are in effect on a particular day concerning a particular subject, it would be necessary to refer both to the appropriate Title(s) of the *CFR* and those *Federal Registers* which contain amendments to the Title(s). This is not as complicated as it sounds. The Office of the Federal Register prepares various finding aids and guides that assist users in determining which issues of the *Federal Register* are needed to update specific regulations.

### When Is the *Code* Published?

The approximately 140 *CFR* volumes are revised at least once a year on a quarterly basis as follows: Titles 1–16 as of January 1; Titles 17–27 as of April 1; Titles 28–41 as of July 1; Titles 42–50 as of October 1.

### Where Is the *Code* Available?

Most law libraries, some public libraries, and all Federal Depository Libraries in major cities have copies of the *CFR*. Individual copies or subscriptions to the entire *CFR* are available from the Superintendent of Documents, U.S. Government Printing Office, Washington, D.C. 20402. Subscription price is $595.00 a year ($743.75 for foreign mailing). Individual copies are separately priced and price inquiries may be made to the Superintendent of Documents of the Office of the Federal Register. For further information call 202-783-3238.

The *CFR* is published by the Office of the Federal Register, National Archives and Records Service, a component of the U.S. General Services Administration.

Source: *Code of Federal Regulations* (Washington, D.C.: U.S. Government Printing Office).

# RULES AND REGULATIONS FOR REGISTERING AS A LOBBYIST

Registering to become a lobbyist requires filing three copies of the Preliminary Report form, one with the secretary of the Senate and two with the clerk of the House of Representatives.

To obtain forms, contact the Secretary of the Senate, Office of Public Records, Hart Building, Suite 232, Washington, D.C. 20510, (202-224-0758). This office will mail sufficient copies of the form, with mailing labels and a copy of the section of the pertinent law.

A.  Who Must Register?

1.  Person(s) who directly or indirectly solicits, collects, or receives money (or any other thing of value) to be used to aid in the passage or defeat of legislation by the United States Congress
2.  Person(s) whose principle function is to aid in the passage or defeat of legislation by the United States Congress

B.  Requirement for Preliminary Report:

1.  Employers and employees must file separate reports.
2.  One copy of the report is to be filed with the secretary of the Senate and two copies are to be filed with the clerk of the House of Representatives.

3. Identifying data:
   a. The name, address and nature of business of employer
   b. Approximate duration of lobbying activities
   c. Statement of general and specific legislative interests:
      1) Short titles of statutes and bills, House and Senate numbers of bills, citations of statutes, and stand (for or against) on such statutes and bills
   d. Description of publications to be received or distributed in connection with legislative interests:
      1) Quantity distributed, date of distribution, name of printer or publisher, and name of donor if publications were a gift
   e. Statement of anticipated expenses:
      1) Nature and amount of expenses and salary of agent or employee

C. Quarterly Report Requirements:
   1. A report must be filed at the end of each calendar quarter (between the first and tenth day) in which money has been received or spent in connection with legislative interest.
   2. One copy of the report is to be filed with the secretary of the Senate and two copies are to be filed with the clerk of the House of Representatives.
   3. Receipts (other than loans):
      a. Gifts of money and printed or duplicated material, and receipts from sales of printed or duplicated material
   4. Loans received:
      a. Total amount presently owed, and amounts borrowed and repaid this quarter
   5. Contributions (including loans):
      a. Name and address of each person who has made a contribution of $500 or more, and the amount contributed
   6. Expenditures (other than loans):
      a. Public relations and advertising services, wages, salaries, fees, and commissions, gifts or contributions printed or duplicated material, office overhead, telephone and telegraph, and travel, food, lodging, and entertainment
   7. Loans made to others:
      a. Total amount presently owed to person filing, lent to others this quarter, and payments received

8. Recipients of Expenditures:
   a. Name and address of recipients of $10 or more, and purpose and date of expenditure

D. Penalties:
   1. A person convicted of violating the provisions of Title III of the Legislative Reorganization Act of 1946 will be considered guilty of a misdemeanor and will be punished by either a maximum fine of $5,000 or a maximum prison sentence of twelve months, or both.
   2. Any person convicted of such a misdemeanor is prohibited from lobbying for three years from the date of conviction; violation of this is considered a felony and is punishable by either a maximum fine of $10,000 or a maximum prison sentence of five years, or both.

Source: Federal Regulation of Lobbying Act (PL. 601) (1946) (Washington, D.C.: U.S. Government Printing Office, 1985).

APPENDIX E

# RULES AND REGULATIONS GOVERNING THE CREATION OF POLITICAL ACTION COMMITTEES

Registering to create a PAC requires filing with the Federal Election Commission (FEC). To obtain the necessary forms, contact the Federal Election Commission, 1325 K Street, N.W., Washington, D.C. 20463 (202–523–4068, or toll free, 800–424–9530). The Commission will supply the copies of the pertinent law and a registration guide and forms.

The Chamber of Commerce of the United States has developed a publication called *Corporate P.A.C. Guidelines.* For copies, write their Publications Department, 1615 H Street, N.W., Washington, D.C. 20062 (202–659–6120). These guidelines at a cost of $50.00 explain the complexities involved in organizing a Political Action Committee.

A. Who Must Register?

   1. A political committee established by a national bank, corporation, labor organization, trade association, cooperative or membership organization, to raise or spend more than $1,000 to influence Federal elections

B. Requirements of Registration (Statement of Organization):

   1. Identifying data:
     a. name and address of the parent organization
     b. name and address of custodian of records, treasurer and assistant treasurer, if any

       c.  mailing address of committee

       d.  officers of committee

       e.  name and address of committee's bank

       f.  name and address of candidate supported by committee, if committee is authorized by a candidate

   2.  Committees must file 10 days after establishment.

C.  Prohibited Contributions:

   1.  Direct campaign contributions by government contractors

   2.  Contributions from foreign nationals who are not permanent residents of the United States

   3.  Other prohibited Contributions include:

       a.  Those made from general treasury funds of a corporation, labor organization or national bank

       b.  Those made by a national bank or federally chartered corporation

       c.  Those made through corporate creditor's forgiveness of political committee's debt

       d.  Those made by discounting merchandise

       e.  Corporate/labor payment for service "rendered on behalf of a political committee." (see page 8 of *Campaign Guide for Corporations and Labor Organizations*

   4.  Contributions of more than $100 per person per campaign

   5.  Contributions made in the name of another person

D.  Contribution Limits:

   1.  Initial limits on Political Action Committees:

       a.  $1,000 per election to a candidate

       b.  $20,000 to a national party committee per calendar year

       c.  $5,000 to any other political committee per calendar year

   2.  An individual can contribute $5,000 to a Political Action Committee per year, $1,000 to each candidate or candidate committee per election, and/or $20,000 to a national party committee per calendar year, for a maximum total of $25,000 per year.

   3.  When a Political Action Committee attains status as a multicandidate committee (committee with more than fifty contributors) and has been registered for at least six

months, and with the exception of State party committees, has made contributions to five or more Federal candidates, then contributions are limited to:
a. $15,000 to a national party committee per calendar
   year
b. $5,000 to any other political committee per calendar
   year. (Contributions between affiliated committees and
   committees of the same party are unlimited.)
c. $5,000 to each candidate or candidate committee per
   election

E. Penalties:
1. A committee found to be in violation of the Federal Election Campaign Act Amendments of 1976 may be required
   to pay a fine not to exceed the greater of $5,000 or an
   amount equal to the amount of the contribution or expenditure involved in the violation.
2. If the FEC has established proof that a Committee was involved in a knowing and willful violation of the Act it may
   be required to pay a fine not to exceed the greater of
   $10,000 or 200 percent of the amount of the contribution
   or expenditure involved in the violation.

Source:  The Federal Election Commission, Washington, D.C.

# SUGGESTIONS FOR
# FURTHER READING

Adams, Gerard, and Lawrence R. Klein, eds. *Industrial Policies for Growth and Competitiveness: An Economic Perspective.* Lexington, Mass.: Lexington Books, 1983.

American Enterprise Institute for Public Policy Research. *Major Regulatory Initiatives During 1980: The Agencies, the Courts, the Congress.* Washington, D.C.: American Enterprise Institute for Public Policy Research, 1981.

Anderson, Ronald Aberdeen. *Government and Business.* 4th ed. Cincinnati: South-Western, 1981.

Ayres, Robert U. *The Next Industrial Revolution: Reviving Industry Through Innovation.* Cambridge, Mass.: Ballinger, 1984.

Bardach, Eugene, and Robert A. Kagan. *Going By the Book: The Problem of Regulatory Unreasonableness.* Philadelphia: Temple University Press, 1982.

____, eds. *Social Regulation: Strategies for Reform.* New Brunswick, N.J.: Transaction Books, 1982.

Bartlett, Bruce R. *Reaganomics: Supply-Side Economics in Action.* Westport, Conn.: Arlington House, 1981.

Behrman, Jack N. *Industrial Policies: International Restructuring and Transnationals.* Lexington, Mass.: Lexington Books, 1984.

Beman, Larry. *The Office of Management and Budget and the Presidency, 1921–1979.* Princeton, N.J.: Princeton University Press, 1979.

Benton, Lewis, ed. *Private Management and Public Policy: Reciprocal Impacts.* Lexington, Mass.: Lexington Books, 1980.

Berenbeim, Ronald. *Regulation: Its Impact on Decision Making.* New York: The Conference Board, 1981.

Berry, Jeffrey M. *The Interest Group Society*. Boston: Little, Brown, 1984.

Bower, Joseph L. *The Two Faces of Management: An American Approach to Leadership in Business and Politics*. Boston: Houghton Mifflin, 1983.

Breyer, Stephen. *Regulation and Its Reform*. Cambridge, Mass.: Harvard University Press, 1982.

Brozen, Yale. *Concentration, Mergers, and Public Policy*. Columbia University Graduate School of Business Studies of the Modern Corporation. New York: MacMillan, 1982.

Buchholz, Rogene A. *Business Environment and Public Policy: Implications for Management*. Englewood Cliffs, N.J.: Prentice-Hall, 1982.

Buchholz, Rogene A., William D. Evans, and Robert A. Wagley. *Essentials of Public Policy for Management*. Englewood Cliffs, N.J.: Prentice-Hall, 1985.

Burch, Philip H. *Elites in American History*. New York: Holmes and Meier, 1980.

Carney, Thomas P. *False Profits: The Decline of Industrial Creativity*. Notre Dame, Ind.: University of Notre Dame Press, 1981.

Cater, Douglas. *Power in Washington*. New York: Random House, 1964.

Center for National Policy. Industry Policy Study Group. *Restoring American Competitiveness: Proposals for an Industry Policy*. Washington, D.C.: Center for National Policy, 1984.

Cigler, Allan J., and Burdett A. Loomis, eds. *Interest Group Politics*. Washington, D.C.: Congressional Quarterly Press, 1983.

Clair, Ken, ed. *Political Action for Business: The PAC Handbook*. Washington, D.C.: Fraser Associates, 1981.

Cochran, Thomas C. *Business in American Life: A History*. New York: McGraw-Hill, 1972.

Collins, Robert M. *The Business Response to Keynes, 1929–1964*. New York: Columbia University Press, 1981.

Committee for Economic Development. Research and Policy Committee. *Redefining Government's Role in the Market System*. New York: Committee for Economic Development, 1979.

Council of State Governments. *Forging Links for a Productive Economy: Partnerships Among Government, Business, and Education*. Lexington, Ky.: Council of State Governments, 1984.

Cronin, Thomas E., and Rexford G. Tugwell, eds. *The Presidency Reappraised*. 2d ed. New York: Praeger, 1977.

Cushman, Robert F., and Herbert A. Morey, eds. *A Guide for the Foreign Investor: Doing Business in the U.S.A.* Homewood, Ill.: Dow Jones-Irwin, 1984.

Davidson, Roger H., and Walter J. Oleszek. *Congress and Its Members*. 2d ed. Washington, D.C.: Congressional Quarterly Press, 1985.

Denison, Edward F. *Trends in American Economic Growth, 1929–1982*. Washington, D.C.: The Brookings Institution, 1985.

Denzau, Arthur T. *Will an "Industrial Policy" Work for the United States?* St. Louis: Center for the Study of American Business, 1983.

Derthick, Martha, and Paul Quirk. *The Politics of Deregulation.* Washington, D.C.: The Brookings Institution, 1985.

Dexter, Lewis Anthony. *How Organizations Are Represented in Washington.* Indianapolis: Bobbs-Merrill, 1969.

Dodd, Lawrence C., and Bruce I. Oppenheimer. *Congress Reconsidered.* 2d ed. Washington, D.C.: Congressional Quarterly Press, 1981.

Dodge, Kirsten, ed. *Government and Business: Prospects for Partnership.* Austin: University of Texas Press, 1980.

Dominguez, George S. *Government Relations: A Handbook for Developing and Conducting the Company Program.* New York: John Wiley and Sons, 1982.

Driscoll, Robert E., and Jack N. Behrman, eds. *National Industrial Policies.* Cambridge, Mass.: Oelgeschlager, Gunn, and Hain, 1984.

Dunlop, John T., ed. *Business and Public Policy.* Boston: Division of Research, Graduate School of Business Administration, Harvard University, 1980.

Eads, George C., and Michael Fix. *The Reagan Regulatory Strategy: An Assessment.* Washington, D.C.: Urban Institute Press, 1984.

_____. *Relief or Reform? Reagan's Regulatory Dilemma.* Washington, D.C.: Urban Institute Press, 1984.

Eells, Richard. *The Political Crises of the Enterprise System.* New York: Collier-MacMillan, 1980.

Ferguson, Allen R., ed. *Attacking Regulatory Problems: An Agenda for Research in the 1980s.* Cambridge, Mass.: Ballinger, 1981.

Fisher, Louis. *Constitutional Conflicts Between Congress and the President.* Princeton, N.J.: Princeton University Press, 1985.

Fox, Harrison W., and Susan Webb Hammond. *Congressional Staff: The Invisible Force in American Lawmaking.* New York: The Free Press, 1975.

Fox, Harrison W., and Martin Schnitzer. *Doing Business in Washington: How to Win Friends and Influence Government.* New York: The Free Press, 1981.

Freeman, J. Leiper. *The Political Process.* Rev. ed. New York: Random House, 1965.

Fritschler, A. Lee. *Smoking and Politics: Policymaking and the Federal Bureaucracy.* 3d ed. Englewood Cliffs, N.J.: Prentice-Hall, 1983.

Fritschler, A. Lee, and Bernard H. Ross. *Business Regulation and Government Decision Making.* Cambridge, Mass.: Winthrop, 1980.

Gatti, James F., ed. *The Limits of Government Regulation.* New York: Academic Press, 1981.

Gies, Thomas G., and Werner Sichel, eds. *Deregulation: Appriasal Before the Fact.* Ann Arbor, Mich.: Division of Research, Graduate School of Business Administration, University of Michigan, 1982.

Goodsell, Charles T. *The Case for Bureaucracy.* 2d ed. Chatham, N.J.: Chatham House, 1986.

*Government Regulation: Achieving Social and Economic Balance.* Studies prepared for the use of the Special Study on Economic Change of the Joint Economic Committee, Congress of the United States. Washington, D.C.: U.S. Government Printing Office, 1980.

Gray, James G., Jr. *Managing the Corporate Image: The Key to Public Trust.* Westport, Conn.: Quorum Books, 1986.

Greenwald, Carol S. *Group Power: Lobbying and Public Policy.* New York: Praeger, 1977.

Gresser, Julian. *Partners in Prosperity: Strategic Industries for the U.S. and Japan.* New York: McGraw-Hill, 1984.

Griffith, Ernest S. *Congress: Its Contemporary Role.* New York: New York University Press, 1961.

Heenan, David A. *The Re-United States of America: An Action Agenda for Improving Business, Government, and Labor Relations.* Reading, Mass.: Addison-Wesley, 1983.

Herman, Edward S. *Corporate Control, Corporate Power.* New York: Cambridge University Press, 1981.

Hessen, Robert, ed. *Does Big Business Rule America? Critical Commentaries on Charles E. Lindblom's "Politics and Markets."* Washington, D.C.: Ethics and Public Policy Center, 1981.

Hochmut, Milton, and William Davidson, eds. *Revitalizing American Industry: Lessons from Our Competitors.* Cambridge, Mass.: Ballinger, 1985.

Hughes, Katherine. *Corporate Response to Declining Rates of Growth.* Lexington, Mass.: Lexington Books, 1982.

Hunker, Jeffrey A. *Structural Change in the U.S. Automobile Industry.* Lexington, Mass.: Lexington Books, 1983.

Hysom, John L., and William J. Bolce. *Business and Its Environment.* St. Paul, Minn.: West, 1983.

Johnson, Chalmers, ed. *The Industrial Policy Debate.* San Francisco: ICS Press, 1984.

Jones, R.J. Barry, ed. *Perspectives on Political Economy.* New York: St. Martin's Press, 1983.

Kaufman, Herbert. *Are Government Organizations Immortal?* Washington, D.C.: The Brookings Institution, 1976.

Koenig, Louis W. *The Chief Executive.* 4th ed. New York: Harcourt Brace Jovanovich, 1981.

Kotz, Nick. *Let Them Eat Promises: The Politics of Hunger in America.* New York: Anchor Books, 1971.

Lave, Lester B. *The Strategy of Social Regulation: Decision Frameworks for Policy.* Washington, D.C.: The Brookings Institution, 1981.

Lawrence, Robert Z. *Can America Compete?* Washington, D.C.: The Brookings Institution, 1984.

Lehmbruch, Gerhard, and Phillippe C. Schmitter. *Patterns of Corporatist Policy-Making.* Sage Modern Politics Series, vol. 7. Beverly Hills, Calif.: Sage Publications, 1982.

LeLoup, Lance T. *Budgetary Politics: Dollars, Deficits, Decisions.* Brunswick, Ohio: King's Court Communications, 1977.

Levine, Charles H. *The Unfinished Agenda for Civil Service Reform: Implications of the Grace Commission Report.* Washington, D.C.: The Brookings Institution, 1985.

Levitan, Sar A. *The Great Society's Poor Law.* Baltimore: Johns Hopkins University Press, 1968.

_____. *Business Lobbies: The Public Good and the Bottom Line.* Baltimore: Johns Hopkins University Press, 1984.

Lindblom, Charles E. *Politics and Markets.* New York: Basic Books, 1977.

Lipset, Seymour Martin, and William Schneider. *The Confidence Gap: Business, Government and Labor in the Public Mind.* New York: The Free Press, 1983.

Litan, Robert E., and William D. Nordhaus. *Reforming Federal Regulation.* New Haven: Yale University Press, 1983.

Lodge, George C. *The New American Ideology.* New York: Alfred A. Knopf, 1975.

_____. *The American Disease.* New York: Alfred A. Knopf, 1984.

McCraw, Thomas K. *Prophets of Regulation: Charles Francis Adams, Louis D. Brandeis, James M. Landis, Alfred E. Kahn.* Cambridge, Mass.: The Belknap Press of Harvard University Press, 1984.

_____, ed. *Regulation in Perspective: Historical Essays.* Cambridge, Mass.: Harvard University Press, 1981.

McGrath, Phyllis S. *Action Plans for Public Affairs.* New York: The Conference Board, 1977.

McKenzie, Richard B. *Bound to be Free.* Stanford, Calif.: Hoover Institution Press, 1982.

_____, ed. *Constitutional Economics: Containing the Economic Powers of Government.* Lexington, Mass.: Lexington Books, 1984.

McQuaid, Kim. *Big Business and Presidential Power.* New York: Morrow, 1982.

Magaziner, Ira C., and Robert B. Reich. *Minding America's Business: The Decline and Rise of the American Economy.* New York: Harcourt Brace Jovanovich, 1982.

Malbin, Michael J. *Unelected Representatives: Congressional Staff and the Future of Representative Government.* New York: Basic Books, 1980.

Manne, Henry G., ed. *Corporate Governance, Past and Future.* New York: K.C.G. Productions, 1982.

Marcus, Alfred A. *The Adversary Economy: Business Responses to Changing Government Requirements.* Westport, Conn.: Quorum Books, 1984.

Marmor, Ted. *The Politics of Medicare.* Rev. ed. Chicago: Aldine, 1973.

Maxey, Margaret N., and Robert Lawrence Kuhn, eds. *Regulatory Reform: New Vision or Old Curse?* New York: Praeger, 1985.

Meier, Kenneth J. *Regulation: Politics, Bureaucracy, and Economics.* New York: St. Martin's Press, 1985.

Meyer, Henry. *The Moving Force.* New York: Amacom, 1981.

Miller, S.M., and Donald Tomas Kovic-Devey. *Recapitalizing America: Alternatives to the Corporate Distortion of National Policy.* Boston: Routledge and Kegan Paul, 1983.

Millstein, Ira M., and Salem M. Katsh. *The Limits of Corporate Power: Existing Constraints on the Exercise of Corporate Discretion.* New York: MacMillan, 1981.

Mitchell, Olivia S. *The Labor Market Impact of Federal Regulation: OSHA, ERISA, EEO and Minimum Wage.* Cambridge, Mass.: National Bureau of Economic Research, 1982.

Mitnick, Barry M. *The Political Economy of Regulation: Creating, Designing, and Removing Regulatory Forms.* New York: Columbia University Press, 1980.

Morrison, Catherine. *Forecasting Public Affairs Priorities.* Research Bulletin No. 192. New York: The Conference Board, 1986.

Mosher, Frederick C. *A Tale of Two Agencies.* Baton Rouge: Louisiana State University Press, 1984.

Moynihan Daniel P. *Maximum Feasible Misunderstanding: Community Action in the War on Poverty.* New York: The Free Press, 1969.

Nagelschmidt, Joseph S., ed. *The Public Affairs Handbook.* New York: Amacom, in association with Fraser Associates, 1982.

Neal, Alfred C. *Business Power and Public Policy.* New York: Praeger, 1981.

Nelson, Richard R., ed. *Government and Technical Progress: A Cross-Industry Analysis.* New York: Pergamon Press, 1982.

Neustadt, Richard E. *Presidential Power: The Politics of Leadership from FDR to Carter.* New York: John Wiley and Sons, 1980.

Noll, Roger G., and Bruce M. Owen. *The Political Economy of Deregulation: Interest Groups in the Regulatory Process.* Washington, D.C.: American Enterprise Institute, 1983.

North, Douglas Cecil, and Roger LeRoy Miller. *The Economics of Public Issues.* 6th ed. New York: Harper and Row, 1983.

Oleszek, Walter J. *Congressional Procedures and the Policy Process.* Washington, D.C.: Congressional Quarterly Press, 1978.

Ornstein, Norman J., and Shirley Elder. *Interest Groups, Lobbying and Policymaking.* Washington, D.C.: Congressional Quarterly Press, 1978.

Perry, James L., and Kenneth L. Kraemer, eds. *Public Management: Public and Private Perspectives.* Palo Alto, Calif.: Mayfield, 1983.

Pertschuk, Michael. *Revolt Against Regulation: The Rise and Pause of the Consumer Movement.* Berkeley: University of California Press, 1982.

Petri, Thomas E., ed. *National Industrial Policy: Solution or Illusion?* Boulder, Colo.: Westview Press, 1984.

Phillips, Keven P. *Staying on Top: The Business Case for a National Industrial Strategy.* New York: Random House, 1984.

Poole, Robert W., Jr., ed. *Instead of Regulation: Alternatives to Federal Regulatory Agencies.* Lexington, Mass.: Lexington Books, 1982.

President's Private Sector Survey on Cost Control. *War on Waste.* New York: Macmillan, 1984.

Quirk, Paul J. *Industry Influence in Federal Regulatory Agencies.* Princeton, N.J.: Princeton University Press, 1981.

_____ . *The Politics of Deregulation.* Washington, D.C.: The Brookings Institution, 1985.

Redman, Eric. *The Dance of Legislation.* New York: Simon and Schuster, 1973.

Reich, Robert B. *The Next American Frontier.* New York: Quadrangle/New York Times Books, 1983.

Richmond, Frederick W. *How to Beat the Japanese at Their Own Game.* Englewood Cliffs, N.J.: Prentice-Hall, 1983.

Ripley, Randall B. *Congress: Process and Policy.* 3d ed. New York: W.W. Norton, 1983.

Ripley, Randall B., and Grace A. Franklin. *Congress, the Bureaucracy, and Public Policy.* 3d ed. Homewood, Ill.: Dorsey Press, 1984.

Rosen, Howard. *Servants of the People: The Uncertain Future of the Federal Civil Service.* Salt Lake City: Olympus, 1985.

Rothwell, Roy, and Walter Zegveld. *Industrial Innovation and Public Policy: Preparing for the 1980's and the 1990's.* Westport, Conn.: Greenwood Press, 1981.

Rourke, Francis E. *Bureaucracy, Politics, and Public Policy.* 3d ed. Little, Brown, 1984.

Rowat, Donald C., ed. *The Government of Federal Capitals.* Toronto, Canada: University of Toronto Press, 1973.

Salomon, Lester M., and Michael S. Lund, eds. *The Reagan Presidency and the Governing of America.* Washington, D.C.: Urban Institute Press, 1984.

Schlosstein, Steven. *Trade War: Greed, Power, and Industrial Policy on Opposite Sides of the Pacific.* New York: St. Martin's Press, 1984.

Schlozman, Kay Lehman, and John T. Tierney. *Organized Interests and American Democracy.* New York: Harper and Row, 1986.

Scott, Bruce R., and George C. Lodge, eds. *U.S. Competitiveness in the World Economy.* Boston: Harvard Business School Press, 1985.

Shamburger, Page. *Tracks Across the Sky: The Story of the Pioneers of the U.S. Airmail.* Philadelphia: J.B. Lippencott, 1964.

Shapiro, Irving S. *America's Third Revolution: Public Interest and the Private Role.* New York: Harper and Row, 1984.

Shipper, Frank, and Marianne M. Jennings. *Business Strategy for the Political Arena.* Westport, Conn.: Quorum Books, 1984.

Siegan, Bernard H. *Economic Liberties and the Constitution.* Chicago: University of Chicago Press, 1980.

Smith, Steven S., and Christopher J. Deering. *Committees in Congress.* Washington, D.C.: Congressional Quarterly Press, 1984.

Steiner, George A. *Business and Society.* 2d ed. New York: Random House, 1975.

Stokes, McNeill. *Conquering Government Regulations: A Business Guide.* New York: McGraw-Hill, 1982.

Stone, Alan. *Regulation and Its Alternatives.* Washington, D.C.: Congressional Quarterly Press, 1982.

Striner, Herbert E. *Regaining the Lead: Policies for Economic Growth.* New York: Praeger, 1984.

Sweet, Morris L. *Industrial Location Policy for Economic Revitalization: National and International Perspectives.* New York: Praeger, 1981.

Thompson, Fred, ed. *Regulatory Regimes in Conflict: Problems of Regulation in a Continential Perspective.* Lanham, Md.: University Press of America, 1984.

Thompson, Fred and L.R. Jones. *Regulatory Policy and Practices: Regulating Better and Regulating Less.* New York: Praeger, 1982.

Thurow, Lester C. *The Case for Industrial Policies.* Washington, D.C.: Center for National Policy, 1984.

Tolchin, Susan J., and Martin Tolchin. *Dismantling America: The Rush to Deregulate.* New York: Oxford University Press, 1983.

Viscusi, W. Kip. *Risk by Choice: Regulating Health and Safety in the Workplace.* Cambridge, Mass.: Harvard University Press, 1983.

Vogel, David. *National Styles of Regulation: Environmental Policy in Great Britain and the United States.* Ithaca, N.Y.: Cornell University Press, 1986.

Vogel, Ezra F. *Comeback, Case By Case: Building the Resurgence of American Business.* New York: Simon and Schuster, 1985.

Wachter, Michael L., and Susan H. Wachter, eds. *Toward a New U.S. Industrial Policy?* Wharton/Reliance Symposium. Philadelphia: University of Pennsylvania Press, 1981.

Weidenbaum, Murray L. *Government-Mandated Price Increases: A Neglected Aspect of Inflation.* Washington, D.C.: American Enterprise Institute for Public Policy Research, 1975.

_____. *Business, Government and the Public.* 3d ed. Englewood Cliffs, N.J.: Prentice-Hall, 1986.

Whitford, Verron, ed. *American Industry.* New York: H.W. Wilson, 1984.

Whynes, David K., and Roger A. Bowles. *The Economic Theory of the State.* Oxford, England: Martin Robertson, 1981.

Wilson, Graham K. *Business and Politics: A Comparative Introduction.* Chatham, N.J.: Chatham House, 1985.

Wilson, James Q., ed. *The Politics of Regulation.* New York: Basic Books, 1980.

Wolfson, Nicholas. *The Modern Corporation: Free Markets Versus Regulation.* New York: The Free Press, 1984.

Zysman, John. *Governments, Markets, and Growth: Financial Systems and the Politics of Industrial Change.* Ithaca, N.Y.: Cornell University Press, 1983.

Zysman, John, and Laura Tyson, eds. *American Industry in International Competition: Government Policies and Corporate Strategies.* Ithaca, N.Y.: Cornell University Press, 1983.

# INDEX

*Achille Lauro* hijacking, 75
Administrative agencies. *See* Agencies
Administrative law justices, 98
Administrative Procedure Act, 97
Advisory Council on Executive Management, 101
Aerospace industry, 48, 113; R&D, 47, 49
Affirmative action, 104
AFL-CIO, 87, 112, 120
Agencies, 93–100, 108–109; accountability, 33; and business, 36–38; and decisionmaking, 73; hearings, 97–100; and interest groups, 93; and lobbyists, 100; longevity of, 125–126; public information offices, 109; reorganization, 117–119; rulemaking, 94–97; and U.S. Congress, 17, 79–80, 95–96
Agriculture, 49–50
Aid to Families with Dependent Children, 139
Air bags, 41
Air pollution, 24, 41
Air traffic controllers, 63
Airline Pilots Association, 144
Airline regulation, 33, 39, 141, 144
Albertine, John, 90
*Almanac of American Politics*, 109

American Airlines, 144
American Automobile Association, 118
American Business Conference, 90
American Enterprise Institute, 67
American Medical Association, 120
American Public Transit Association, 118
Americans for Constitutional Action, 109
Americans for Democratic Action, 109
Amtrak, 143
Apollo project, 34
Appropriations committees, 71, 72, 137
Ash, Roy, 12
Ash Commission, 101
AT&T, 33, 39
Atlantic Richfield Company, 4
Authorization committees, 71–72
Auto seat belt interlock, 72
Automobile industry, 50; fuel efficiency standards, 130; protectionism, 51; regulation, 35, 41
*Aviation News*, 110

Bail-outs, 2
Baker, James, 103
Balance of payments, 6

Balanced Budget and Emergency Deficit Control Act, 138
Banking and securities regulation, 2, 26, 33, 39, 46, 141, 144–145
Bankruptcies, 2
Bargaining, 124–127
BIPAC, 87
Birnbaum, Jeffrey, 142
Blumenthal, W. Michael, 11–12
Boeing, 41
Brock, William, 104
Budget, 51, 136–140, 146
Bureau of the Budget, 104, 135
Bureaucracy. *See* Agencies; Civil service
Business and government, 1–7, 133; and future, 141–147; and lobbying, 87–90; *see also* Corporations
Business Industrial Political Action Committee, 87
Business Roundtable, 25, 40

Cabinet councils, 103–104, 135
Cabinet secretaries, 14–15, 74
*Calendar of Federal Regulations*, 33
*Calendars of the United States House of Representatives and History of Legislation*, 155–156
Camp David Accords, 75
Campaign finance laws, 87–89; *see also* Political action committees
Campbell, Alan K., 10, 20 n. 3
Cancer research, 125, 131
Carter, Jimmy, 11; attack against bureaucracy, 65, 67; and deregulation, 33, 40; and domestic policy, 103; and education department, 118; and energy policy, 129–130, 131; and foreign policy, 75; and Occupational Safety and Health Administration, 114
Caucuses, 84–85
CEOs and government, 3–4, 40
*Chadha* case, 100
*Challenger*, 13, 19, 113
Chandler, Alfred, 2
*Chronicle of Higher Education*, 110
Chrysler, 47–48
Cigarettes, health warnings on, 116–117
Cities, deterioration of, 131–132
Civil rights regulation, 24, 38

Civil service, 57–67; attacks against by politicians, 65–67; executive level, 60, 62–63, 67; firings, 64–65; morale, 67; number of employees, 57–61; reforms, 61–63; retirement system, 63–65
Civil Service Commission, 20 n. 3, 62
Civil Service Reform Act, 62
Civilian Conservation Corps, 129
Client groups, 14, 15–16
Clothing industry, flammable fabrics, 38
Cloture, 157
Coalition building, 117
*Code of Federal Regulations*, 98, 99, 169–171
Combustion Engineering, 41
Commerce and Trade Council, 103
Committee on Political Education (COPE), 87
Common Cause, 25
Community services block grant, 143
Concurrent resolutions, 154
Conference Board, 4, 146–147
Confidence in government, 66
Congressional Budget and Impoundment Control Act (1974), 136–137
Congressional Budget Office, 46, 48–49, 80, 134; creation, 136; and Grace Commission, 135; and Gramm-Rudman-Hollings, 139
*Congressional Directory*, 109
*Congressional Quarterly*, 82, 110
*Congressional Quarterly Almanac*, 108
*Congressional Record*, 82, 111
Congressional Research Service, 63, 80
*Congressional Staff Directory*, 109
*Consent Calendar*, 155
Conservation, 15
Consumer Product Safety Commission, 32, 100
Consumer protection, 25, 32, 100
COPE, 87
Copyrights, 24, 46
Corporations, 3–4, 141–147; financial assistance from government, 47–49; objectives, defining, 19–20; public distrust of, 66, 141, 145; regulation, 25, 36–41; and tax reform, 48; Washington offices, 4, 25; *see also* Business and government
Cram, William C., 53

Credit programs, 48, 49
Current account balances, 145

Data collection, 50
Decisionmaking systems, 71–76, 112–115, 123; and agencies, 73; alternative, 115–121; and big issues, 127–133; and lobbyists, 82–87; locating, 107–110; and political action committees, 87–90; and president, 74–75; reform, 134–140; tracking, 110–112; and U. S. Congress, 76–81, 136–140
Deficit, 51, 146
Democratic party, 88
Democratic Study Group, 84
Denison, Edward F., 31, 52
Deregulation, 2, 32–36, 143–145; and politics, 39–41; *see also* Regulation
*Discharge Calendar*, 156
District of Columbia, 80, 115–116
Domestic Policy Council, 72, 75, 85, 101–102, 104
Drug Enforcement Caucus, 84
Drug regulation, 2, 24, 114, 133

Eastern Airlines, 144
Economic Affairs Council, 103
Economic Development Administration, 14, 143
Economic Opportunity Act of 1964, 119–120
Economic regulation, 23, 25–26
Education, 54, 73, 118; employment in, 60
Electrical equipment manufacturers, 49
Elementary and Secondary Education Act, 143
Ellwood, John, 137
Employment discrimination, 24, 25, 32
Endangered species, 24
Energy, 74, 118–119, 127–128, 129–130, 146; regulation, 26, 33, 38
Entitlement programs, 136
Entry barrier, government regulation as, 37
Environmental Protection Agency, 32, 35–36; employees, 60
Environmental regulation, 24, 26, 141, 146; costs, 32; and deregulation, 35; and oil industry, 38

Equal employment opportunity, 24, 32, 38
Executive office of the president, 100–105, 108; publications, 165–167
Expertise, 76, 93–95
Export-Import Bank, 48, 50
Export promotion, 49–50
Externalities, 26

Farm subsidies, 145
Farmers Home Administration, 15
Federal Aviation Agency, 144
Federal Communications Commission, 95
Federal Election Campaign Act of 1971, 87–88
Federal Highway Administration, 118
Federal Labor Relations Board, 62
Federal Power Commission, 130
*Federal Register*, 97, 98–99, 111, 165–167, 170
Federal Trade Commission, 37, 60, 100
Financial assistance programs, 47–50
Firing government employees, 15
First Continental Bank of Chicago, 47–48
Flammable Fabrics Act of 1967, 38
Flood, Daniel, 77
Food and Agriculture Council, 103
Food and Drug Administration, 114
Food purity regulation, 2, 24, 37, 114
Food stamps, 16, 117, 139
Ford, Gerald, 102; and civil service, 67; and deregulation, 33, 40
Ford Motor Co., 9, 142
Foreign competition. *See* Protectionism
Foreign policy, 75
Franklin, Grace A., 120

General Accounting Office, 74, 80, 134, 136; and Grace Commission, 135
General Electric, 4
General Motors, 142
GI Bill of Rights, 131–133
Glenn, John, 130
Grace, J. Peter, 9, 17
Grace Commission, 9, 16–17, 134–135
Gramm-Rudman-Hollings, 138

Great Depression, 128–129
Gross national product, government
    expenditure as percentage, 3, 49, 143

Hamilton, Alexander, 44
Harris poll, 66
Hart, Gary, 89
Hay Associates, 64
Head Start, 143
Health policy, 70
Health regulation, 26, 32
Hearings: agencies, 97–100; and U.S.
    Congress, 13, 109, 154
High-tech industry, 53
Highway programs, 133
*House Calendar*, 155
House Republican Study Committee,
    84
Housing programs, 16, 73, 131–133
Human Resources Council, 103
Human services programs, 16

Impoundment, 136, 137
Industrial policy, 44, 50–55
Inflation: and deficit, 51; indexing,
    64; and regulations, 31–32
Infrastructure responsibilities of
    government, 46
Insurance industry, 41
Integrity and Efficiency Council, 135
Interest groups, 72, 75, 128; and
    agencies, 93; and industrial policy,
    52; and lobbyists, 83–85, 86; and
    regulation, 25
Interest rates, 32, 51
Internal Revenue Service, 97
Interstate Commerce Commission, 26
Investment tax credit, 48
Issues management, 4

Japanese auto imports, 51
Jefferson, Thomas, 5
Johnson, Lyndon B., 115–116; and
    civil service, 61, 67
Johnson and Johnson, 114
Joint resolutions, 154
Jones, Reginald, 3–4

Kaufman, Herbert, 125–126
Kentucky Resolutions, 5
Keyworth, George A., 47
Koenig, Louis W., 45

Labor, 50, 54
LaFalce, John J., 146
Law enforcement personnel, 63
Legal Policy Council, 103
Legal Services Corporation, 143
Legislative Reorganization Act of
    1946, 81–82
Legislative Reorganization Act of
    1970, 158–159
Legislative veto, 99–100
Levine, Charles, 63
Licenses, awarding, 23, 97–98
Lindblom, Charles E., 45, 124
Litton Industries, 12
Lobbyists, 54, 81–87; and agencies,
    100; and decisionmaking, 69, 75;
    and interest groups, 83–85, 86;
    number of, 81; registration of,
    82–83, 173–175; and regulation, 25,
    36, 39–41; resources, 85–87; and
    tracking decisionmaking, 111–112;
    and U.S. Congress, 82–85, 86–87
Local government, 25, 73; employee
    growth, 58–60
Local Government Caucus, 84
Locke, John, 4–5
Lockheed, 47–48
Lodge, George C., 4–5, 53
*Los Angeles Times*, 145

Majority leader of the Senate, 77
Management and Administration
    Council, 103
Management Improvement Council,
    135
Maritime Administration, 14
Market, response to, 1–2, 5
Mass transit, 73, 133
Media, 13, 73; specialized 110, 11
Medicaid, 139
Medicare, 119, 120
Meese, Edwin, 103–104
Mencken, H. L., 40
Merchant Marine, 14
Merit Systems Protection Board, 62
Miller, Arjay, 9
Mining industry, 49
Mobil Oil Company, 4
Money supply regulation, 24, 46

NASA, 13, 18–19; contractors, 113;
    product ideas, 48; R&D, 47

National Association of Manufacturers, 25, 39, 112
National Bureau of Standards, 14
National Council of Senior Citizens, 120
National debt, 127; *see also* Deficit
National Education Association, 118
National Federation of Independent Business, 142
National Fire Prevention and Control Administration, 14
*National Journal*, 81, 110
National Labor Relations Board, 62
National Oceanic and Atmospheric Administration, 14
National Park Service, 69
National Realty Committee, 89
National Resources and Environment Council, 103
National Science Foundation, 47
National Security Council, 101, 103
Natural gas price regulation, 33, 129, 130
New Federalism, 142
Newsletter, 110
Nixon, Richard M., 67, 101–102, 104, 142
Nuclear energy industry, 38
Nutrition programs, 117, 139; *see also* Food stamps

Objectives, defining, 19–20
O'Brien, John, 144
Occupational Safety and Health Administration, 32, 60, 114
Office of Cabinet Affairs, 103
Office of Management and Budget, 12, 72, 101, 104–105; and decision-making, 75; and deregulation, 35; and government reform, 135, 139; and lobbyists, 85
Office of Personnel Management, 10, 62
Office of Planning and Evaluation, 103, 104
Office of Policy Development, 103
Office of Technology Assessment, 80
Offshore oil leases, 130
Oil depletion allowance, 51
Oil price deregulation, 33
Older Americans Act, 143
Older industries, protection of, 52

Omnibus Trade Bill, 146
Openness and government, 12–13
Ornstein, Norman, 67

PACs. *See* Political action committees
Party caucuses, 77
Patent and Trademark Office, 14
Patents, 2, 24, 46
Pay equity, 25, 32
Pell college scholarship grants, 143
Pennsylvania Society for the Promotion of Manufacturers and Useful Arts, 44
Personnel costs and regulation, 32
Phillips, Kevin, 54–55
Planning Program Budgeting System (PPBS), 134
Plant closings, 147
Pluralism, 124–127
Political action committees (PACs), 87–90, 177–179
Postal Rate Commission, 18
Presidents: councils, 103–104, 135; and decisionmaking, 74–75; executive office, 100–104, 108, 165–167; veto, 162–163
President's Private Sector Survey on Cost Control. *See* Grace Commission
*Private Calendar*, 155–156
Private law, 163
Procurement policies of government, 3, 32, 49
Production costs and regulation, 32
Productivity, 19–20, 145–146
Productivity Improvement Program, 135
Professional associations, 83
Property rights, 5, 24, 46
Protectionism, 21, 51–52, 145–147
Proxmire, William, 129–130
Public confidence in government, 66
Public goods, 141
Public Health Service, 69
Public interest groups. *See* Interest groups
Public law, 163
Public sector management: difficulties of, 16–19; vs. private sector management, 9–20
Public service jobs, 143

Railroads regulation, 26, 33
Reagan, Ronald, 15; and aerospace program, 48; appointments, 61; and budget, 138; and bureaucracy, 65–66, 67, 126–127; cabinet councils, 103–104; and deregulation, 33–36, 40; and economy, 142–143; foreign policy, 75; and government employment, 58; and government management, 9, 16; and R&D expenditure 47; and tax reform, 128
Regan, Donald T., 103
Regional development commissions, 143
Regulation, 1, 23–41; business response to, 25, 36–41; classes of, 24–31; costs and effects, 31–32, 33; employment in agencies, 60; and lobbyists, 82–83, 173–175; public response to, 66, 141; and social policy, 24, 26–31, 35, 38–41; and state government, 25; see also Deregulation
Regulatory Council, 33
Reich, Robert B., 52–53
Reorganization Act of 1939, 101
Republican party, 88
Research and development, 47, 49
Resolutions, 154
Ripley, Randall B., 120
Roosevelt, Franklin D., 45, 129
Roper Organization poll, 145
Rotation of government personnel, 13–14

Safety standards, 2, 25, 32
Sayre, Wallace, 9
Secretary of agriculture, 15
Securities and Exchange Commission, 60, 129
Semiconductor industry, 49
Senior Executive Service (SES), 62–63
Small business, 33, 45
Small Business Administration, 48, 143, 145
Smith-Connally Act, 87
Social policy considerations, 18; and business, 38–41; and regulation, 24, 26–31, 35, 38–41
Social security, 32, 128–129; and budget, 139; government employees, 64

Social Security Administration, 20
South Africa, 147
Space shuttle. See Challenger
Speaker of the House, 77, 154, 157, 162
Stanford Graduate School of Business, 9
State government: decisionmaking, 73; employment growth, 58–60; industrial policies, 53; regulations, 25
State of the Union message, 102
Steiner, George, 3, 10
Student loan program, 145
Subsidies, 2, 18
Supplemental Security Income, 139
Supply-side economics, 127
System diagram, 100–111

Tax policies, 48, 54; reforms, 89, 128, 141–142
Teachers, 60
Telecommunications regulation, 26, 33, 39, 144
Teller vote, 158
Textile industry, 51
Third-party delivery of government service, 63
Thurber, James A., 137
Time, 81
Tobacco price supports, 125, 131
Toxic waste program, 36
Trade associations, 4, 108
Trade policies, 49–50, 70, 128, 130–131; see also Protectionism
Trade publications, 110
Trademark protection, 46
Transistor radios, 37
Transportation industry regulation, 26, 33
Trucking industry deregulation, 33, 39
Tylenol poisonings, 114

Unemployment insurance, 32
Union Calendar, 155
Unions, 108
Unisys, 11
U.S. Chamber of Commerce, 39, 112, 142, 177
U.S. Code, 108
U.S. Conference of Mayors, 118
U.S. Congress: and agencies, 17, 79–80, 95–96, 99; and budget,

136–140; and committees, 76–77, 78, 154–155; conferences, 159–162; confirmation of presidential appointees, 60, 61; debates, 156–157; decisionmaking, 76–81, 136–140; energy program, 129–130; hearings, 13, 109, 154; industrial policy, 51; legislative calendars, 155–158; and lobbyists, 82–85, 86–87; reform, 77–78; retirement benefits, 63. staff, 78–79, 84, 109; subcommittees, 71–73, 74, 75, 76, 78, 108, 109, 154; voting, 157–158
U.S. Constitution, 5–7, 46; and division of powers, 69; and lobbying rights, 81, 82; and management systems, 112
U.S. Department of Agriculture, 15–16, 95–97; education program, 118; export promotion, 50; and food stamps, 117; regulatory costs, 32
U.S. Department of Commerce, 14, 50, 54, 131
U.S. Department of Defense, 49; civilian employees, 57–58; education, 118; R&D, 47
U.S. Department of Education, 118
U.S. Department of Energy, 118–119, 130
U.S. Department of Health and Human Services, 74
U.S. Department of Housing and Urban Development, 76, 80, 119
U.S. Department of the Interior, 130
U.S. Department of State, 50
"U.S. Department of Trade," 54, 131
U.S. Department of Transportation, 130

U.S. Department of the Treasury, 11
U.S. Forest Service, 15
U.S. Government Manual, 108–109
U.S. Postal Service, 17–18, 65, 73; and air mail, 48; civilian employees, 57–58; public attitude toward, 66
U.S. Supreme Court, 100
Universities, 25, 107
Urban development action grants, 143
Urban Mass Transit Administration, 118

Veterans Administration, 57–58, 69
Veto, 162–163
Vinson, Carl, 77

War on Poverty, 119–120
Washington, D.C.: civil service employees in, 75, 88; corporate offices in, 4, 25
Washington Board of Trade, 116
Watergate scandals, 87, 100
Weather Bureau, 14
Weidenbaum, Murray, 32
White House Office, 75, 101
White House Office of the Special Trade Representative, 50
Whitten, Jamie L., 117
Wilson, Graham K., 51
Women's organizations, 25, 38
Workmen's compensation, 32
Works Progress Administration, 129

Youth Conservation Corps, 143

Zero-Based Budgeting (ZBB), 134

# ABOUT THE AUTHORS

**A. Lee Fritschler** is President of Dickinson College in Carlisle, Pennsylvania. He was the director of the Center for Public Policy Education at The Brookings Institution. Before joining Brookings he was chairman of the U.S. Postal Rate Commission, appointed by President Carter. A former dean and professor of government and public administration at American University, Fritschler has taught business-government relations, public administration, intergovernmental relations, and policy analysis. He has held academic appointments as assistant to the dean of the Maxwell Graduate School; visiting lecturer, College of William and Mary; director of the National Center for Education in Politics, American University; faculty fellow, International Institute of Social Studies, The Hague; and guest professor at the University of Cologne. Dr. Fritschler holds master's and Ph.D. degrees from The Maxwell School of Citizenship and Public Affairs, Syracuse University. He has written extensively on bureaucratic policymaking, the problems of metropolitan government, and government regulation.

**Bernard H. Ross** is professor and chairman of the department of public administration at the American University. He has directed several programs and institutes at American University, including the Center for Urban Public Policy Analysis, the Urban Affairs Program, the Urban Affairs Institute, the NASPAA Urban Administration Fellows

Program, the Urban Careers Program, and the American Political Science Association's State and Local Government Internship Program. Dr. Ross has also developed and administered executive training programs for major corporations as well as senior executives at the federal, state, and local levels. He holds a B.S. in economics from The Wharton School and an M.A. and Ph.D. in government from New York University. He has published widely on urban politics and metropolitan problems.